Solving the Financial Investing and Trading Puzzle

www.financialinvestingandtrading.com

SOLVING THE FINANCIAL INVESTING AND TRADING PUZZLE

Gill and Michael Fielding

New Generation Publishing

www.financialinvestingandtrading.com

We would both like to thank Dr Mark Nugent for travelling some of this journey with us!

Contents

www.financialinvestingandtrading.com

7. Tier Five

Foreword

Somewhere in the middle of 2016, my son Michael, having just finished his zoology degree, said to me 'so what's all this share trading about then?'

Well, Michael, this is our answer!

In order to find out and answer that basic question, Michael and I have been on a year long journey to discover what we can learn about share investing and trading and this is the result – a strategy and guidebook for anyone to follow in order to achieve a steady 10% return on small amounts of money which, if properly invested, will create financial freedom for most people and most families over time.

Our learning journey has been taken together as a mum and son – we've attended all courses together for instance and throughout the writings we have used I/we interchangeably. Sometimes the I is Michael and sometimes it's me.

We've also used £ and $ fairly indiscriminately. These strategies work whenever you are and whatever your local currency might be and we invest in both the USA and the UK for instance – but we could invest anywhere in the world from our desk at home. We've identified a couple of share brokers who between them cover more or less the entire globe – so again, it doesn't matter where you live or what currency you start with – these strategies are entirely possible for you!

We've used only two currencies to demonstrate: US dollars or sterling, although any currency will do, and we use the two currencies to generally mean either and if it matters which one it is we will say so.

Finally, you will see that we have dated each week of our learning over one year 1st May 2017 – 30th April 2018. We've left in the dates so that you can see our progress but it matters not one jot when you start – as long as you do start! You will also see that out of the full year we've taken 10 weeks off for holidays because we don't want this to be a full time activity for us, and we take regular breaks, but you can create your own year to suit you and your circumstances.

Enjoy your own journey!

Gill Fielding

JILL (FULL LENGTH)

Preface: April 15th 2017

I heard on the UK TV this morning two pieces of news:

Item One

A report of a junior teacher, who qualified in a class of 37 people, of whom only 7 are still teaching 5 years later, because the others have all left the profession due to non-classroom time workload (form filling and backside protection) and impact on their mental health.

Apparently 1 in 5 parents are now being asked to set up automated regular payments to their child's school to pay for basic 'stuff'.

I know this second item to be true as my own daughter is a primary school teacher and they don't have money for paint. Her school has sent a letter to parents saying if they want their child to do painting, they have to send in £1 for paints.

I also know that schools often 'manage out' older, more experienced teachers, as they are the more expensive ones who hit the school budgets hard, and they of course are replaced with cheap resources: newly qualified and inexperienced teaching staff.

Item Two

Last Wednesday on my BBC radio show we discussed a reported item about nurses, some of whom have to stop patient care to go and move their cars every two hours because there is insufficient parking for them at the hospital. Over time, nurses' accommodation has been used for hospital functions: car parks are inadequate and apparently at my local hospital the nursing staff are forbidden from parking on site and have to park elsewhere and get bussed in.

We know that the NHS in the UK is short of at least 5,000 general practitioners: and that in 2016 50.4% of junior doctors who finished the two year foundation training stayed in the NHS. Rather shockingly, that's a massive drop on the year before when 71.3% stayed in the NHS. There's clearly a problem there.

Two items of news: one about the UK education system and one about the health system. I could go on with a different story about UK state pensions (one of my usual hobby horses!), library closures, rubbish collection, or housing shortages – but you get the point, I hope. This country is struggling to pay for the services we seem to have become accustomed to getting: and it will only get worse.

Nor are we alone. Although I am quoting issues for the UK here, this is a global phenomenon. More than half of U.S. households risk being unable to maintain their standard of living in retirement. The US Social Security is due to run short of money by 2033 and about a third of US workers aren't offered retirement plans. I could quote similar stories for most countries as budgets are tighter across the whole world and I worry about how future generations will cope with a diminishing or a completely absent level of governmental financial support for any of the world's health or educational services.

In an unpredictable and increasingly turbulent world, what can we do? Well there are two schools of thought: we either give up and do nothing or we do something, and I've always been a woman of action so I'm on the do something side.

But what?

I can't do anything personally about BREXIT or Donald Trump's policies: I can't single-handedly fund any health care or education system: as an individual I can't elect or dethrone any one person of power, so I can't worry about any of that.

What I can do though is to take responsibility for the things I CAN do something about, and protect my family as best I can. I can provide for their present and their future such that if a time comes when they need medical care, or refuge or a house on top of a hill because global warming has caused rising sea levels – then they have the money to do that and save themselves.

I don't actually think in reality anything cataclysmic is going to happen to the world as humans have a habit of being sensible when it really matters. I'm an optimist at heart and I have faith in human kind, but I do think that times are going to get tougher and tougher financially for the average family and I want to do my best to enable me and my children (and their children) to live a life of relative ease without financial worry.

I KNOW I can do that, because I have a lifetime of experience of wealth creation under my belt, but that wealth creation has happened mainly in the property arena, and although I have a lot of financial discipline and awareness, I don't have any substantial experience in share trading or investing. I've dabbled of course. I've always had a 'few bob' in shares, and I know a bit about the financial world and how shares work. That gives me personally a head start.

My son Michael however is 22, a recently graduated zoology student and knows almost nothing about shares. He's a boomerang child and has recently moved back in with me, although that's about to change as he's about to move in with some friends again. Like most graduates, he hasn't been able to find his niche yet, or a proper full-time job. In short, he's normal!

Therefore, I think we're suitably poised for a social and financial experiment!

The experiment

We want to see if we, a normal mum and son family pairing, and with little or no experience, can understand how to create wealth using shares as the basic financial vehicle.

For us, we've set ourselves a year to learn and to take some appropriate action. Our year runs from the 1st May 2017 to the 30th April 2018 and our objective is to be able to invest and to generate approximately 10% per year return on anything we invest in.

Our initial target is to do this for one year but I know that if we can do that for one year, we will be able to do it for two and three and onwards.

I also know that if we can achieve that base 10% increase then our financial future is secured because of the magic of simple strategies added to compounding.

Evidence

We will report on the key information and create our 'lessons and learnings' as we go along so that you too can follow those simple steps.

We are going to record our thoughts as we go along and they will be available on the website so you can follow our journey. www.financialinvestingandtrading.com

We will also do regular summaries of where we've got to: half term reports and annual statements will be downloaded so you can see, and they too will be available on the website.

Conclusion

I know for absolutely certain that if Michael and I can do this, so can any parent/child, friends and family group, or individual – and that's all we need to secure the financial future of any family, and protect us all from the future challenges yet to come.

Financial Introduction: Starting Capital

In an ideal world it would be best to start this exercise with a lump sum of money but it is perfectly possible to start with a small monthly savings amount. However, we are both fortunate in that we have some money to start with: I personally have some old corporate pension money that I can use for investment and Michael has a little nest egg that his mum created for him!

My collection of old company pensions has now been transferred into a Self Invested Personal Pension arrangement (a SIPP in the UK) and as at May 1st 2017, my SIPP is worth £188,216.13.

There are equivalent self-administered and self-investing schemes in most territories globally such as the 401k in the USA.

Then, Michael has had the benefit of £50 per month from his parents paid every month from when he was born until he was 18. This was paid into a tax efficient programme for children that was worth about £36k when he reached 18. He has yet to do anything with that, because he can't just spend it (that was part of the deal!) and he can't withdraw the money until he's 55 (under current legislation) but he can add to it and invest it more or less where he likes.

Therefore, for the purposes of this experiment he has transferred that money into the same SIPP arrangement as my money. That transfer cost a little in fees and so to start this experiment Michael had £35,773.14.

Regular Savings and Compounding

I'd just like to go off on a detour here and talk about that simple savings mechanism that I set up for all my children the minute they were born.

In the UK a parent receives a child benefit allowance from the Government which is paid monthly from birth until they are 18, unless they leave full-time education earlier. When my children were born – basically in the 1990s' – this amounted to approximately £50 per month per child. Nowadays I understand it's nearer to £90 per month.

We decided as soon as the children were born that it was better to put that away for their future than to spend it on short-term stuff. Therefore, when Michael was born in December 1994 we started a savings plan for him.

Try this exercise yourself: go to www.thecalculatorsite.com and insert a monthly savings amount, a rate of return and a period of savings – then press the calculate button to see how a small amount of money compounds over time.

Here's the projection for Michael's child benefit savings money!

Compound Interest Calculator

 Use my popular calculators to work out the **compound interest on your savings**, with monthly interest breakdowns and the option to include regular monthly deposits or withdrawals (for retirement calculations, etc). Use the second calculator to work out interest on a simple lump sum savings amount. You can find out the formula for compound interest here.

| REGULAR DEPOSIT / WITHDRAWAL | STANDARD CALCULATOR |

CURRENCY:	Pound (£) ▼
BASE AMOUNT:	£ 50
ANNUAL INTEREST RATE:	11 %
CALCULATION PERIOD:	18 years ▼
REGULAR MONTHLY?	£ 50 deposit ▼
INCREASE DEPOSITS/WITHDRAWALS YEARLY WITH INFLATION?	◼
COMPOUND INTERVAL: ?	Daily ▼

Calculate

(interest compounded **daily** - added at the end of each day)

Year	Year Deposits	Year Interest	Total Deposits	Total Interest	Balance
1	£600.00	£42.96	£650.00	£42.96	£692.96
2	£600.00	£117.71	£1,250.00	£160.68	£1,410.68
3	£600.00	£201.15	£1,850.00	£361.83	£2,211.83
4	£600.00	£294.30	£2,450.00	£656.13	£3,106.13
5	£600.00	£398.27	£3,050.00	£1,054.39	£4,104.39
6	£600.00	£514.32	£3,650.00	£1,568.72	£5,218.72
7	£600.00	£643.88	£4,250.00	£2,212.59	£6,462.59
8	£600.00	£788.49	£4,850.00	£3,001.08	£7,851.08
9	£600.00	£949.91	£5,450.00	£3,950.99	£9,400.99
10	£600.00	£1,130.10	£6,050.00	£5,081.10	£11,131.10
11	£600.00	£1,331.25	£6,650.00	£6,412.34	£13,062.34
12	£600.00	£1,555.77	£7,250.00	£7,968.12	£15,218.12
13	£600.00	£1,806.40	£7,850.00	£9,774.52	£17,624.52
14	£600.00	£2,086.17	£8,450.00	£11,860.69	£20,310.69
15	£600.00	£2,398.46	£9,050.00	£14,259.15	£23,309.15
16	£600.00	£2,747.06	£9,650.00	£17,006.21	£26,656.21
17	£600.00	£3,136.19	£10,250.00	£20,142.40	£30,392.40
18	£600.00	£3,570.56	£10,850.00	£23,712.95	£34,562.95 ✳

The projected outcome after 18 years of child benefit savings was a staggering £34,562.95!

I decided to save that money into a pensions type of environment (which you can do for a child as soon as they're born) – and the longer you can save for the future the smaller the amount you need to save.

And at the end of the 18 years Michael's savings were actually worth £36,160!

Stakeholder Pension Plan

Yearly statement no. 11, for the year ending 27 Mar 2013

MICHAEL P FIELDING

Chosen retirement date: 28 December 2049, age: 55
Date of birth: 28 December 1994

Your plan summary

We've sent this statement to help you review your plan for retirement.
This page summarises the key information about your plan. The rest of
the statement gives more detailed information.

Single payments, transfer payments or instructions given to us up to 3
working days before your yearly statement date may not be included in
your current and forecast final plan values. These payments are however
included in the payments sections.

Your plan value

Current value on 27 Mar 2013	£36,160.83

Regular Saving and Compounding Summary

It's one of those magical truths, that small amounts of money regularly saved, compounded and left for a relatively long time will turn into a large amount – eventually!

Whether you're lucky enough to receive a £50 allowance from the Government or not, PLEASE start a regular savings pot as early as you can, for yourself and your children.

The results speak for themselves – DO IT!

Experiment Summary

All the information you need about this and all the other information you need to follow our journey for yourself is available on the website, and in the following chapters. The information is also available in an online module – for more information go to: www.financialinvestingandtrading.com

1. Introduction

Week One: 1st – 7th May 2017

LESSONS and LEARNINGS

Fundamentally, we want to be able to do this wealth creation alongside our other lives and neither of us want it to be time intensive.

However, I think we may need to give it some thought in the early days and so I'm going to allocate about 10 hours this week to get this experiment started. Although I don't intend for this experiment to be anywhere near so time intensive for me when I get rolling.

I currently don't know how to invest or what I'm going to invest in, but having successfully created wealth both in property and in business I know that I need to get clear on a vision or plan. Whilst I'm learning about the 'how to' I need to know what I'm aiming at. So I need a year-long vision and strategic plan.

I'm going to start with a plan of my share Pyramid strategy:

The Basic Strategy

As with any investment portfolio, it pays to diversify and we need to have a share investing strategy to cover different requirements, strategies and attitudes to risk,

1

and there are many different ways of making money from shares.

UNLIKE some investments such as property, shares do not easily fit neatly into alternating tiers of income generation and capital lump sums. If you bought a share for £1 and sold it for £1.20 within one month does that mean you've created income or capital? In the main we would define that as a capital gain but we can use it as income if we wish.

As a guide it may be easier to split investments into two categories:

INVESTING – where we are buying shares to hold for a relatively long-time for capital growth for our future. These shares are for the long term, for the rainy day, and may be held ideally in an ISA (Individual Savings Account) or pension where there are some tax perks too, but any savings pot will do. Share investing in this case is done **IN**frequently and takes less time to monitor or maintain.

AND,

TRADING – where the activity is more like a business done with the intention to make regular profits or income. Share trading tends to be done more frequently, in this case and needs more attention and maintenance. In general, share traders need more specialist skills and knowledge.

The Share Pyramid: Overview

Trading: For Example
Fancy Pants, Options, Dividend Chasing

Capital: Holding for Value
Long-term buy & hold strategy – fundamentals

Long-term Investing
Regular long-term savings: Collective Compounding Investment Schemes, ISAs

Top Level Trading

Trading

Daily Action

Buy & Hold

Simple Capital Strategies - SIPPs

Regular Savings: Cappuccino: ISA

Trading: Regular Action
Regular daily action: Shares, Indices or Currencies

Capital Investing
Simple capital strategies, year on year - SIPPs

We can use the simple structure of the Pyramid to create a share portfolio strategy, as follows:

Tier One at the bottom is this long-term, very diversified approach to share investing. Ideally these investments are in tax-free savings environments, like pensions or in a self select ISA. Ideally, you start saving and investing here as a child – or for your children. Investments made here are left for many years with little to no input or monitoring.

Tier Two is another capital, long-term investment tier and would involve investing in a well-established and proven strategy such as the O'Higgins strategy where you invest in a very small selection (normally 5 shares) in a large index like the Dow Jones in America or the FTSE in the UK. When applied, this principle is called the 'Dogs of the Dow' or the 'Beat the FTSE' strategy. At time of writing the 5 'Small Dogs' (see more later) – have generated a 10.4% return per annum between 2000 and 2016. The UK version has generated an average annual 12.2% over the last 15 years. This strategy is only looked at once a year, so is NOT time intensive.

Tier Three involves more activity as an investor as it involves stock picking for long-term increases in value. This can either be done with a recommendation from a data provider or broker, or can be done by yourself where you look at the corporate fundamentals that establish a shares value. This is sometimes called the Buy and Hold Strategy.

Tier Four is about more active trading of any tradable item: shares, commodities or currencies and involves trading off information about the share price, and how it moves. This can be done with trading systems or data such as charts, stochastics, Fibonnaci waves, or MACD. It is less important WHAT you trade (shares, commodities or currencies) and is more about HOW you trade, WHAT indicators you use and WHY you buy and sell.

Tier Five is everything else! I include in here all the 'Fancy Pants' type of trading that you should NOT do until you have proper education and support and I include in this tier:

- Any derivatives trading
- Complicated options trading
- Strategies like stock splits, and
- Day, short term or swing trading
- Dividend Chasing

In summary it looks like this:

20% +	Trading / Daily Action
12 – 15 % +	Buy & Hold
10 – 12 % +	Simple Capital Strategies - SIPPs
8 – 10 % +	Regular Savings: Cappuccino: ISA

The Pyramid, Tiers Timings and Risk

Pulling all those pieces of information together will create a strategic plan for any would-be share investor.

At the very bottom in Tier One, we invest very little, and generally invest regular savings of about £50 - £75 per month. The risk here is minimal; we can stop it quickly if we need to but the aim is to leave it for many years without touching anything: so set up a Direct Debit for the monthly savings amount and just let time fly by and create wealth! You can leave these funds for many years and if you're doing this for your children, then perhaps leave it for 18 years!

At Tier Two we are taking a little bit more risk and with a little bit more money and over a shorter time period. It isn't really worth investing in Tier Two unless you have about £2k to start with. If you only have £2k then start with the 5 'Dogs of the FTSE', then when you have another £2k add the 5 from the 'Dogs of the Dow'. If you have £4k then do those two together, then add the next 5 from the FTSE and the next 5 from the Dow. Overall, if you did all that then you could invest from £8k here (or much much more if you wish). This strategy needs to be looked at once per year.

At Tier Three we need slightly more input and slightly more time to watch it. We would need to research the fundamentals and make a decision. Ideally, you wold invest at least £500 in each share you want to invest in and it would need checking every month or so.

At Tiers Four and Five you risk much less and very little financially but you invest a lot more in terms of time. Any decent strategy at this level would require daily input of say, 10–30 minutes but you would only risk say 0.5% of your pot of money at any time.

Overall then, the Pyramid provides a complete balance of risk, reward and time input, as well as a structure for learning, development and changes in financial circumstances.

It can provide a structure for a lifetime of investing and trading!

To download your own copy of the Pyramid click on: www.financialinvestingandtrading/Pyramid.

Conclusion

This is a "clear" overview of our plan or strategy, we now need to explore and learn about each of these tiers in much more detail – and that is our "one year's" learning. Now we have that big picture of our year's activity both in terms of learning AND in terms of investments

Diary

Gill: It's both exciting and daunting to think that were at the start of a year long 'journey' here but I know for certain that this is doable! I also know that we don't need any fancy software or subscriptions – but we do need the Pyramid strategy as well as some targets and detailed plans - so that's what I'll concentrate on next.

Michael: I struggle with planning quite a lot so this structure really helps me focus.

Week Two: 8ᵗʰ – 14ᵗʰ May 2017

LESSONS and LEARNINGS

We now have a broad idea of my strategy for the year and now we need to set some targets and plans.

Let's look at the broad target of 10% per year growth. How realistic is it?

The Basic Target

The basic target for annual growth with any of our investment strategies is always 10%: and that is a feasible target for share investing.

If we look at share values over the last 25 years we see a meteoric overall growth:

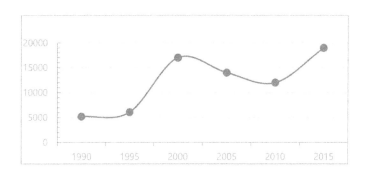

If we look even longer over 50 years, we find even greater growth:

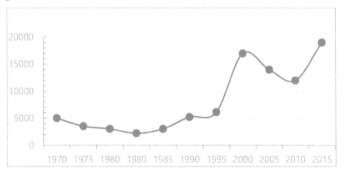

Chart from www.stockmarketalmanac.co.uk

It's interesting how the peaks and troughs that seem extreme, in the shorter 25 year graph, don't look so scary in the second 50 year chart, even though the rises and falls would have been similar. Clearly, the longer our perspective or measure is, the less those ups and downs are noticeable and the less they hurt emotionally. Any short-term movement which seems dramatic on the day, looks far less so with the perspective of time.

It really **does** pay to look at this long-term. Not only is it better for the assessment of sustainable returns but it's also far better for your emotional health!

I've also included two different types of UK share analysis: the FTSE 100 and the FTSE All Share – these are described in the definitions section – and for the moment I am using a variety of different share groupings, both UK and US to show you a broad picture.

But what's the annual return?

The answer is: it depends on exactly what you measure and when you start that measure and end it.

For example: If we take the FTSE 100 (the biggest 100 shares in the UK) for instance. The index began on 3 January 1984 at the base level of 1,000; the highest closing value reached to date is 7,103.98 on 27 April 2015 and the highest intra-day value (at the time of writing) was 7,129 on 11 October 2016. So, it depends on what day – and what time of day – you sell your shares. If we just take the first and last dates here and extrapolate those figures, they broadly create a compounded rate of return of just under 7% per year.

Also, it depends on whether we account for inflation (most prudent) or not, and if we do, these are the returns by country over the whole of the 20th century.

Annual Equity Returns After Inflation During the 20th Century: Dr. Bryan Taylor,

Country	1899-1949	1949-1999
Australia	9.31%	6.98%
France	0.03%	8.14%
Germany	-5.38%	9.29%
Italy	-2.36%	5.25%
Japan	-11.12%	18.73%
United Kingdom	2.13%	8.23%
United States	4.84%	9.21%
World	2.81%	8.53%

As you can tell there is a variation in exactly how much a share will increase in value but we have a couple of pieces of evidence here that suggest it's at least 7% and possibly nearer to 9% if we look at the Annual Equity Returns for the world between 1949–1999.

Also, these figures are just averages and contain the whole gamut of shares in all sorts of companies. With a little bit of simple stock selection (which we will look at shortly) to ensure we pick (broadly) the shares that are most likely to increase in value, rather than the entire cross section of corporate ups and downs, we can be fairly confident of the 10% return.

These are long-term trends of course and for our Fielding Financial customers we have a couple of simple strategies that even children can do: one that tracks the overall stock market, such that you get returns like these above; and one that has created a return that far exceeds it. We've included these later in this book.

If we look at the US market (and any UK investor can invest in these shares just as easily as they can the UK-based ones), we can see that over about 80 years US groups of shares rose between 9.7% and 12.4% annualised – and with all dividends re-invested.

The following are 10-year annualized percentage returns for the S&P 500 Index, U.S. Large Cap Value, U.S. Small Cap and U.S. Small Cap Value. Returns are in percentages.

DECADE RETURNS 1930 THROUGH 2009

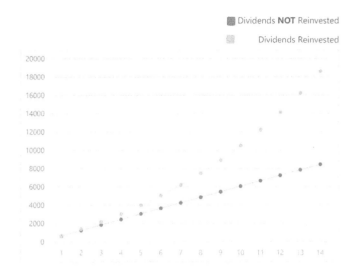

Graph reproduced from www.marketwatch.com

There are TWO key points to note here:

1) Reinvesting the income or dividend from the shares makes a massive difference. Remember the compounding mentioned earlier? The 10% growth is only achieved if all dividends are reinvested, and

2) Understand that these are long-term results: you will see from all the charts above that there are up years and down years and it's only if you invest over the long term that you can achieve them!

NOTE: US versus the UK stock market. Overall the US and the UK stock markets (and any major market like the Japanese, or the German) perform in very similar ways and with very similar returns but the US always has more statistics and charts than the UK (I guess we just don't

13

shout about our performance in the same way), and in any case you can invest anywhere in the world via your armchair so either market is equally available to you. Therefore, if it's easier or clearer to use evidence from other markets then let's use that.

Advanced targets

We are very comfortable using 10% as a target for the bottom three tiers of the Pyramid but we know that if we are going to put in any significant time and effort on the Tiers 4 and 5, we need to get a higher return than that – and again we are very confident that we can – once we have the knowledge!

Daily Diary

Gill: I'm already getting frustrated with all this planning and targeting when I want to INVEST! Of course, all the planning means I have more chance of success but I'm itching to start.

Michael: I like that all of this can be done in front of my laptop as I spend most of my time there anyway!

Week Three: 15th – 21st May 2017

LESSONS and LEARNINGS

The Personal Plans! - Gill

Now we have some strategic outlines we need to apply those to our individual personal circumstances.

As I'm older (late fifties at the time of writing) and need to protect my pension as much as possible, I have decided, certainly for the beginning in any case, to stick to the bottom two tiers of the Pyramid: the base level of Collective Investments (The Cappuchino Factor) and then the simple 'Dogs' strategy from Tier Two.

My understanding is that I can get 10% from those two tiers with little time input from me, so I've set my outline strategic plan as follows:

1) My plan is going to cover 25 years which will take me to the age of 84. I've taken that as the average age of my parents: my mum passed away when she was 78 and my dad Reg is still going at 90: the middle of those two is 84 so I'm going to assume I can live that long! If I live longer, my intention is that my pension pot will still be running sufficiently.

    (I've quickly just checked on my spreadsheet and on the assumptions I'm using, my money will run out when I'm 104, so I feel pretty safe with that).

2) I've assumed that I will work for another 10 years and make the maximum contribution I currently can of £10k per year. Interestingly, this contribution (*called the Money Purchase Annual Allowance [MPAA] – and is the amount you can put into a pension once you've made an initial withdrawal – which I did a few years ago to buy a property*) was reduced to £4k per annum part way through our year long experiment but I did manage to get the full amount of allowance invested in year one, before the reduction came into force!

N.B. My contribution is going to be made via one of my companies, as that's where my money is! However, this means that the company gets the tax relief (and quite right too) and not me personally. If I made that contribution personally then I would pay in say, £80 to my pension then the Revenue (HMRC in the UK) would put in the tax relief of £20 directly into the pension. With a corporate contribution, the company puts in £100 and then gets a £20 refund on its corporation tax.

ALL numbers are approximates only, and will vary from country to country. IF you want to make your investing through a pensions vehicle then please contact your own local Revenue service for information about relevant allowances.

3) I've assumed that I will get a 10% gain on my shares: but I've deducted from that growth 1% for share trading and investment costs.

4) I've assumed that the costs I currently pay for my fund (SIPP) management of £239 per year increase by 10% per annum. There was a "one off" set up fee of £678 which was incurred in year one.

5) Then I've assumed that I will start drawing 10% of my pot for the final 15 years of my 25 year plan.

6) I've assumed that all gains, contributions and costs will occur exactly on the 30th April in each year which of course, isn't true but the peaks and troughs of the impact of variable dates will offset one another.

> **The results of all that are that I will turn my £188,216.13 into a NET pot (after annual withdrawals) of roughly half a million at £498,334 over 25 years. That'll do me!**

N.B. I know if I die before the age of 75 this SIPP pension pot will go to my children tax-free, which is a bit of a conundrum really as I didn't fancy dying that early just as a tax wheeze! However, the tax rules in the UK are still generous if I pass away after the age of 75, as my children will then be able to draw that pension at THEIR marginal tax rate at the time.

Here's my summary spreadsheet:

Gills Pension	Data:	Growth %	10
		Fee Increase %	10
		Withdrawal %	10
		Contribution	£10,000

Date	Starting balance	10% Growth	Contribution	Fees	Total	Withdrawal
01/05/2017	£188,126.13	£18,624.49	£10,000.00	-£678.00	£216,072.62	
01/05/2018	£216,072.62	£21,391.19	£4,000.00	-£238.00	£241,225.81	
01/05/2019	£241,225.81	£23,881.35	£4,000.00	-£261.80	£268,845.36	
01/05/2020	£268,845.36	£26,615.69	£4,000.00	-£287.98	£299,173.07	
01/05/2021	£299,173.07	£29,618.13	£4,000.00	-£316.78	£332,474.43	
01/05/2022	£332,474.43	£32,914.97	£4,000.00	-£348.46	£369,040.94	
01/05/2023	£369,040.94	£36,535.05	£4,000.00	-£383.30	£409,192.69	
01/05/2024	£409,192.69	£40,510.08	£4,000.00	-£421.63	£453,281.14	
01/05/2025	£453,281.14	£44,874.83	£4,000.00	-£463.79	£501,692.17	
01/05/2026	£501,692.17	£49,667.53	£4,000.00	-£510.17	£554,849.53	
01/05/2027	£554,849.53	£54,930.10		-£561.19	£609,218.44	£60,921.84
01/05/2028	£548,296.59	£54,281.36		-£617.31	£601,960.65	£60,196.06
01/05/2029	£541,764.58	£53,634.69		-£679.04	£594,720.23	£59,472.02
01/05/2030	£535,248.21	£52,989.57		-£746.95	£587,490.84	£58,749.08
01/05/2031	£528,741.75	£52,345.43		-£821.64	£580,265.55	£58,026.55
01/05/2032	£522,238.99	£51,701.66		-£903.80	£573,036.85	£57,303.68
01/05/2033	£515,733.16	£51,057.58		-£994.19	£565,796.56	£56,579.66
01/05/2034	£509,216.90	£50,412.47		-£1,093.60	£558,535.77	£55,853.58
01/05/2035	£502,682.20	£49,765.54		-£1,202.96	£551,244.77	£55,124.48
01/05/2036	£496,120.29	£49,115.91		-£1,323.26	£543,912.94	£54,391.29
01/05/2037	£489,521.65	£48,462.64		-£1,455.59	£536,528.70	£53,652.87
01/05/2038	£482,875.83	£47,804.71		-£1,601.14	£529,079.40	£52,907.94
01/05/2039	£476,171.46	£47,140.97		-£1,761.26	£521,551.17	£52,155.12
01/05/2040	£469,396.05	£46,470.21		-£1,937.39	£513,928.88	£51,392.89
01/05/2041	£462,535.99	£45,791.06		-£2,131.12	£506,195.93	£50,619.59
01/05/2042	£455,576.34	£45,102.06		-£2,344.24	£498,334.16	£49,833.42

If you want to use my planning spreadsheet for your own purposes – go to this website for the download link www.financialinvestingandtrading.com

Extra thought

It's occurred to me how important timing is and how important it is to get all dividends and interest re-invested immediately so that the fund gets the maximum benefit of compounding.

Stress Testing the Strategic Plan

I've assumed the 10% model of growth, fee increase and withdrawal to get to my £498k, but if I put in more optimistic figures of 12% growth, 5% fee increase and then 10% withdrawal my initial £188,126 turns into £807,674 when I'm 84.

Most importantly, the plan provides me with an annual income of over £50k (before tax) at the lower level and £80k per year on the more optimistic predictions more or less for ever!

Because the growth and the withdrawal amount are very similar each annum, this fund will continue to run almost undiminished for ever, therefore I can make decisions about withdrawing a higher amount as I get older and leaving less to my children or I can spend less and leave more – it's a choice I will have that many won't!

In summary:

Probable outcome   a fund of £498,334 at age 84
Better outcome   a fund of £807,674 at age 84

Overall then I think that plan fits my criteria and I'm OK with that (but if I wasn't, I could just change my strategic plan!).

Daily Diary

Gill: I know that the Strategic Pyramid contains 5 levels or Tiers and I have 12 months to learn it all, so I'm assuming I will allocate 2 months of my next year to learning each Tier – and then have two months off! That sounds like a reasonable plan when I'm also busy doing other things.

Michael: Thanks to the time I've got left to invest, my spreadsheet says I'll make millions, so I just need to get on with it.

Week Four: 22nd – 28th May 2017

LESSONS and LEARNINGS

The Personal Plans! Michael's

Now, Michael is 22 and has a completely different strategy to me. Although we're both going to follow the same Tiered Pyramid structure, he won't be able to withdraw any of his money from his SIPP for many, many years to come.

This pot of money that Michael is starting with is in the same SIPP pension structure as mine, and he will only be able to withdraw any of it (unless the legislation changes, of course) when he retires. At the moment, for his type of pension that's the age of 55 and that age will rise to 57 in 2028 and I suspect it will keep rising beyond that – so for the purposes of this exercise I've assumed that he won't be able to get his hands on any of the money until he's 67!

However, what that means is that his money has a very long to grow, and his initial £35,773.14 will grow to an absolutely staggering £1,968,850 by the time he's 67 (in 2062) on the assumption that he creates a 10% annual return, pays his (ever increasing SIPP annual fees) and doesn't add or subtract anything in that time.

Now that's not bad but he can do much better.

If he has another two year break from making any contributions (there's been nothing paid in since he was 18) but he then starts making a small £50 per month contribution (annual contribution of £600) in  2019 and keeps that up each year, it increases his pension pot to an amazing £2,246,466.22.

This is fantastic because, as a person of working age, if he makes that contribution of £600 per year the tax man (HMRC) will add tax relief to that at Michael's personal tax rate – which let's assume is the basic rate of 20% – to make £750 per year invested.

It's worth saying that all again and slowly. A simple savings scheme started by his mum when he was born, with contributions made until the age of 18 and then continued from the age of 25 at only £50 per month can provide a retirement pot of £2.25 million!

Here's the spreadsheet:

Michael's Plan with Contributions	Fee increase %	10				
	Withdrawal %	10				
	Contribution	£600				

Date	Starting balance	10% Growth	Contribution	Fees	Total	Withdrawal
01/05/2017	£35,773.14	£3,541.54	£0.00	-£298.00	£39,016.68	
01/05/2018	£39,016.68	£3,862.65	£0.00	-£327.80	£42,551.53	
01/05/2019	£42,551.53	£4,212.60	£750.00	-£360.58	£47,153.55	
01/05/2020	£47,153.55	£4,668.20	£750.00	-£396.64	£52,175.12	
01/05/2021	£52,175.12	£5,165.34	£750.00	-£436.30	£57,654.15	
01/05/2022	£57,654.15	£5,707.76	£750.00	-£479.93	£63,631.98	
01/05/2023	£63,631.98	£6,299.57	£750.00	-£527.93	£70,153.62	
01/05/2024	£70,153.62	£6,945.21	£750.00	-£580.72	£77,268.11	
01/05/2029	£112,796.78	£11,166.88	£750.00	-£935.25	£123,778.41	
01/05/2053	£953,560.44	£94,402.48	£750.00	-£9,211.98	£1,039,500.95	
01/05/2054	£1,039,500.95	£102,910.59	£750.00	-£10,133.18	£1,133,028.36	
01/05/2055	£1,133,028.36	£112,169.81	£750.00	-£11,146.49	£1,234,801.68	
01/05/2056	£1,234,801.68	£122,245.37	£750.00	-£12,261.14	£1,345,535.90	
01/05/2057	£1,345,535.90	£133,208.05	£750.00	-£13,487.26	£1,466,006.69	
01/05/2058	£1,466,006.69	£145,134.66	£750.00	-£14,835.98	£1,597,055.37	
01/05/2059	£1,597,055.37	£158,108.48	£750.00	-£16,319.58	£1,739,594.27	
01/05/2060	£1,739,594.27	£172,219.83	£750.00	-£17,951.54	£1,894,612.57	
01/05/2061	£1,894,612.57	£187,566.64	£750.00	-£19,746.69	£2,063,182.51	
01/05/2062	£2,063,182.51	£204,255.07	£750.00	-£21,721.36	**£2,246,466.22**	
01/05/2063	£2,246,466.22	£222,400.16	£750.00	-£23,893.50	£2,445,722.88	

It just goes to show how powerful compounding over a fairly long time can be with quite small amounts of money.

And this is the main reason we are doing this year long experiment. If we can create a future fund of this size for Michael then we could do it for every child being born: this could be the way that we solve the pension crisis that we have both in the UK and across the world.

If we could just deflect £50 per child from the government's budget (or perhaps split the current £90 monthly child benefit so half goes to the parent and half to this pension fund scheme), then every child could have what Michael is going to have.

Clearly, if you don't start this savings programme the day the child is born, the overall fund would be less but at least we would all be able to have something and the provision of pensions to all wouldn't be bankrupting countries across the globe.

This will enable people to create some financial independence and to protect themselves against the challenges of the future, and the paucity of national government support. In addition, it enables some economic strength: if every family can provide for their future and their children's and grandchildren's future, it removes a crucial burden from any state worldwide.

Now who knows what Michael's money will be worth, or be able to purchase, in 45 years' time, but fundamentally, as long as the investment return of 10% is higher than the rate of inflation (currently about 2-3% in the UK and the USA) then his money will ALWAYS be worth more in the future than it is today so that's a positive and encouraging thought.

In addition, it will be a £2.25 million pot that he wouldn't have had otherwise and it will certainly help.

Also, sadly, it will be a £2.25 million pot that many others will NOT have unless they take the same action.

Personal Plans: Summary

Michael and I are completely different: he is young, has time on his side and not very much money. I'm older and have a little stashed away but need a pension soon.

Michael aims to input as little as possible over a long period of time whereas mine is to create something quickly, but we are both building a financial future on the 10% model: mine is £10k in per year, 10% growth and 10% withdrawal, and Michael's is more simply based on 10% growth.

Our joint experiment intends to prove that whoever you are and whenever you start – there will always be some way to create a financial fund for your future.

However, there is a big assumption here – and that's the fact that in order to achieve this people need to take responsibility for their finances and acquire the necessary knowledge. These lessons and modules will provide the knowledge – all we all need to do now is to take the action needed!

Daily Diary

End of month one

Gill: Well it's been a busy month. I've had a lot of other stuff as well as this but I've managed to set the strategic plan, the 10% target and my personal plan on what to invest and when to withdraw.

And I've learnt some good stuff! I now know about DRIP shares, and a bit more about taxation and pensions, and most importantly, I know if I can get Michael going with this, he can build a pension pot of about £2m quite easily.

Of course the next task for Michael – once he's got this under his belt – is to sort out his two sisters, who also have the same pension pot invested by me since they were babies, and neither of them know what to do with it yet!

Michael: I feel great about the plan ahead and so far nothing's been too tricky. I'm looking forward to starting to make £2.25 million but even at a low estimate it seems like a no brainer. I definitely need to start telling people about investing once I know how it's done. This seems especially important to tell young people so that they can have hope of one day retiring comfortably.

2. Tier One

Week Five: 29ᵗʰ May – 4ᵗʰ June 2017

LESSONS and LEARNINGS

Tier One – so what's a share then?

There are many different terms banded about in the stock market. Sometimes we call it stock or equity or shares but fundamentally a share is just that – a share – normally of a company.

The ownership of a company is divided into little parcels and these are shares. Sometimes there are only one or two shares and sometimes there's millions but if you own a share you own one brick in the wall of that business!

That share is normally a portion of a company. A company (in the UK) can either be private or public.

A private company normally has the LTD. suffix and a public one has PLC. (Public Limited Company).

In the US there are similar, but not identical distinctions. Companies in the US are normally either a LLP (Limited Liability Company) or a Corporation, and they have slightly different ownership structures.

As you can trade more or less any larger company shares from or in almost any country then it doesn't really matter what you trade but rather "how" and "why". In most of our strategies we trade both UK and US currencies (or euro, Japan and so on).

The fundamental difference in the UK is that a private company is owned privately and the only way you can buy a share is to buy it from the current owners directly, whereas public company shares are available to buy and sell in a public places and quite easily.

Normally those public shares are also traded on a stock market in the country in which it is registered. The price of the shares is quoted on that market. With some very big companies (like Coca-Cola for instance) the shares are quoted on several of the world's largest stock markets across the globe.

Stock Markets

A stock market is purely a 'shop' in which shares can be easily bought and sold – or exchanged (hence the term stock exchange) and at a given published price.

Most stock markets are regulated by their respective governments.

The oldest stock market in the world is the Amsterdam Stock Market which traded shares from 1602, (although there is a record of shares being traded in Antwerp from about 1531). However, neither Antwerp nor Amsterdam are major players in today's investing world.

The older, most established markets nowadays are:
- The UK (London)
- USA (New York)
- Other major European cities such as Paris, Frankfurt, Milan (now all part of the European Stock Market)
- Some Asian markets: (including Hong Kong, Singapore and Japan.)

As you can probably see all of these markets are north of the Equator!

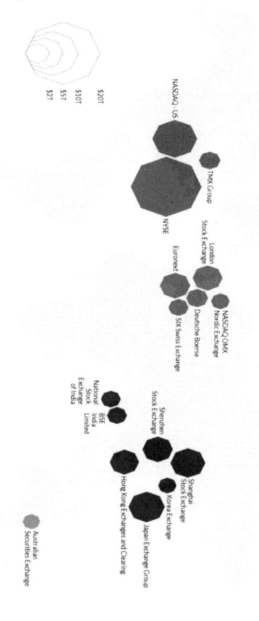

There are some major market south of the Equator – but not many!

When trading or investing it is best to stick to major reputable stock markets, where the market is regulated, where it is easy to move your money in and out, and easy to convert to and from their base currency.

Fortunately, there are plenty of those!

Indices

Within each stock market a long list is available of the shares that can be bought and sold there – in fact, it's just like any other business catalogue or brochure detailing what's available.

On stock markets these lists are called indices. Most markets have lots of lists as they break the overall list of potential shares into sub groups and categories.

In the UK there are many hundreds of different indices published by FTSE.

FTSE is named after the publication that first published these lists of shares and stands for the Financial Times Stock Exchange. Similarly, in the US the main indices were first published by an organisation called Dow Jones and Company.

These should both sound familiar!

There are approximately 630 companies quoted or listed on the UK stock market and they are normally divided as follows:

FTSE All share
FTSE 100 (the top 100)

FTSE 250 (the next 250)
FTSE 350
FTSE Small Cap

In the USA the main indices are:

The Dow Jones Industrial Average ('The Dow') – the top 30 stocks

The Nasdaq 100 (actually the top 107 non-financial stocks)

NYSE Composite Index (the entire list)

S&P 500 Composite Stock Price Index (a composite index of 500 companies covering a cross-section of all sectors, sizes etc on the NYSE).

All stock markets have their own lists or indices.

Stock Market returns

We have evidence that over time the value of shares rises and if we look at the value of the main stock markets overall we can see quite a rise:

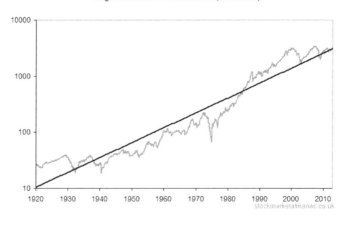

Long-term trend of FTSE All Share (1920-2013)

www.financialinvestingandtrading.com

Long-term trend of the Dow Jones Industrial Average (1913 - 2012)

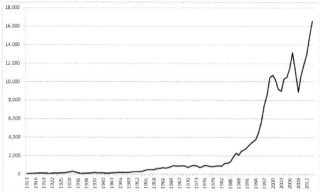

Figure 1: Dow Jones Industrial Average priced in nominal U.S. dollars

It makes sense then that if we could invest in the entire stock market itself then the value of our shares would also rise.

But that's very difficult to do – and very expensive!

But we can invest in the index itself – either as a straightforward trade, which we will cover at the Tier Four level of our learning – or in a tracker fund, which we will look at next.

www.financialinvestingandtrading.com

Daily Diary

Gill: I'm finding all this fascinating. I love looking at the history and derivation of our global financial markets. It also makes me realise that most of this is quite easy and when you pull it apart, most definitions and terms are easy to grasp and understand. I like it!

Michael: seeing how the stock market has continued to rise overall despite recessions and crashes makes me much more confident that I can get returns by investing in it.

Week Six: 5th – 11th June 2017

LESSONS and LEARNINGS

Tier One: Tracking the Index

We now know that each stock market has a long list of possible shares to buy and sell and that list is known as an index. In the UK it's known as the FTSE All Share Index. It can be broken into a variety of sub groups which are just different parts of the overall list or index.

We also now have evidence that over time (and in major markets like the UK and the USA) the value of shares rises and very roughly this is approaching 10% per annum over a hundred years or so. Within that long term result there are clearly disaster years and boom years, so we have to look very long-term to see that level of return – and we suggest 10 years for starters!

That's a great return and far exceeds anything we could achieve in bank deposits or fixed interest bonds therefore, it makes sense that we want to get access to that.

Now we could do that by going shopping with a very big basket and buying ONE of each share in an index – but that would be hugely complicated, very very expensive (as you'd be paying not only the price of each share but also the transaction charge on every share purchase!).

Fortunately, there are two easier ways to buy all the shares in an index:

a) A tracker fund (which is a Tier One investment), and

b) Trading the index as an entity in itself (a Tier Four trading activity).

We will cover both methods and for now we'll start with the easiest way – buying a tracker fund.

Tracker Funds

A tracker fund is one that tracks or mirrors a particular group of shares and the most common are those that track an index like the Dow or the FTSE. However, a tracker fund could track a market sector, say, pharmaceuticals or a particular industry like the automobile trade, a geographical area, like Asia or a specific group such as small technical start up businesses: there are many thousands of trackers to choose from.

At this Tier One level we will look at tracking a particular index partly because it's easier and partly because that will cover the broadest spread of shares in our investing pot which has the effect of spreading the risk to its lowest level and this also gives us a greater degree of certainty.

If an index makes 10% in one year we are almost certain that the tracker fund will also make 10%. There is no real danger of making less than that or underperforming the index. HOWEVER, there is little chance of outperforming it either.

What a tracker fund will give us is predictability and

long-term gains (as long as the stock markets continue to rise as they have for a hundred years or more); what they won't give us is *above* average returns (that part comes later!).

Our first task then is to choose an index to track and at this level of investing choose a large one! The FTSE All Share or the S&P 500 – what you need is an index with a broad spread and large numbers of shares.

For the sake of demonstration, I will look for a fund that tracks the FTSE All Share and I will start by logging onto a comparison website that list, compares and monitors tracker funds. In the UK an example of that is:
www.trustnet.com

In the US for instance these funds are either mutual funds or EFTs and you can information about them on broker websites such as TD Ameritrade.

How to choose a fund: UK

1) From the home page of the www.trustnet.com website, click or hover over the investments button and choose passive funds.

2) Choose UK equities: click on that and then there will appear a list of 50 or so potential funds. That's too many to choose from so to refine the search click on the grey "refine" box and select FTSE All share.

3) That reduces the choice to about 20, so refine further by clicking on the legal structures: check Unit Trust (a generic flexible fund vehicle).

4) Then you can also check the passive rating and the top rating is 5 crowns in this system, check that and you will be left with a handful of options:

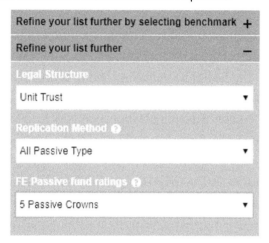

5) There are two extra things to look for: the OCF (far right column in the fund list). This stands for Ongoing Charges Figures and this needs to be as low as possible. The typical fund OCF will be less than 0.5% and hopefully about 0.1% – so very low.

6) Finally, click on the performance tab for the funds and the remaining funds will then be listed in order of performance. As they are tracker funds they should all be very similar.

As at the date of writing they show a standard performance for the FTSE over 1 year of 12.43% and a 3 year performance of 34.54% (so 11.51% average per year). This is based on the current market so can fluctuate.

Alongside the performance figures there is a

Performance over 1yr	Benchmark perf over 1yr	1yr tracking difference	Performance over 3yrs	Benchmark perf over 3yrs	3yrs tracking difference
12.60	12.43	0.16	33.72	34.54	-0.82
12.53	12.43	0.10	33.29	34.54	-1.25
12.64	12.43	0.21	32.82	34.54	-1.72
12.88	12.43	0.45	34.70	34.54	0.16
12.86	12.43	0.42	34.74	34.54	0.20

separate column showing the benchmark and that is the performance of the Index selected and then there's a difference between the two columns.

They are normally all very similar at this stage but there might be one fund that outperforms the others.

7) At this stage any fund will do, so put a pin in the list or choose one randomly and then write down the EXACT fund details (each fund manager may have several funds all with very similar names so you need to get the right one).

8) Make sure that the fund you have chosen offers accumulation units (often labelled 'acc' in the fund title or description) so that any earnings get automatically accumulated or compounded up. We need 'acc' units rather than income units where dividends are paid out.

9) Then click on the fund title or the fund manager name and that should then take you through to a page showing the website, e-mail and phone number of the fund concerned. Now make that call, or email and start investing!

We call this strategy the Cappuccino Factor because the broad aim of this is to invest a fairly small amount of money regularly over a long period of time and all we need is the cost of a cappuccino per day to make it work. As a broad brush, allocate £/$ 50 per month.

Therefore, when you contact the fund manager, make sure that they do allow regular savings at your particular level.

Then all you do is pop a few £/$ into a savings box every day and then invest that monthly and watch your money grow!

There are two important things to note:

1) I casually mentioned the return rates – see the table above – 12.34% over 1 year and 34.54% over 3. Not bad at all! If we could just grow our money at that rate for a few years our initial target would easily be met.

2) I have used Trustnet here as our comparison site and have described it as it looks today. However, you may be looking for funds that track an index from the USA or Asia for instance, and in any case, websites are always changing.

So just put 'tracker fund comparisons' into your search engine and take the principles from the instructions above to create your own selection process that works for the territory or website you're in.

Daily Diary

Gill: There is something very satisfying about tracker funds: it's the certainty of what's going to happen - and that relieves any pressure. All you do is plonk the money in and the system and market does the rest. EASY!

Michael: I'm staggered by the rates of return for something so simple – 10% for doing pretty much nothing. I'll take that.

Week Seven: 12th – 18th June 2017

LESSONS and LEARNINGS

Tier One: Tracking the Index – regularly!

We now know that as long as an investment fund tracks exactly what an index is doing that we will achieve the same results as the index itself (more or less) so our result will be as good – or as bad – as the index and no more.

This is also a very basic regular long term saving strategy, what the regular savings element of the strategy also does is to even out the price and the risk even further, and this is known as pound – or dollar – or euro – cost averaging.

A simple example will illustrate:

Let's invest $/£100 per month for 5 months, obtaining the following prices for each share or unit:

Month One	1.00
Month Two	0.75
Month Three	1.00
Month Four	1.25
Month Five	1.00

Our logic and instinct tells us that our average price of purchase over the five months has been 1.00 per share because we've had three months at a price of 1.00 and one month 0.25 lower and one month 0.25 higher, but is the average really 1.00?

Month	Price	Investment £/$	No. of shares Purchased
One	1.00	100	100.00
Two	0.75	100	133.33
Three	1.00	100	100.00
Four	1.25	100	80.00
Five	1.00	100	100.00
	TOTALS	500	513.33

The average cost of each share has been:
    500/513.33 = 0.97

....and not 1.00 and if I were to sell them today then I would make:
(cost of 1.00 – 0.97) 0.03 * 513.33 (the number of shares)
profit = 15.40
over my starting capital of 500.

It's obvious that this is a better result than investing all £/$500 at one time at 1.00 per share and the regular saving has had the result of averaging down our cost price.

Our final profit is going to be the end value at the time we sell less the accumulated cost price of all the shares and so the lower the cost price of our shares or units the better.

It makes sense then that if the price drops we could buy loads of shares at that time to bring down our average cost of purchase overall and then make even more money when it goes back up – but that would involve watching the market and the fundamentals and predicting that the price was going to go up – and that's a set of skills we can learn at a later stage.

It's true that if we were to buy ALL our shares at the lowest price (i.e. the 0.75) then our profit would be the highest but that would involve timing the market and knowing the individual share (and the company) itself intimately.

For now we can accept that the small regular savings approach does have an averaging benefit.

The investments we make at Tier One of our Pyramid are meant to be simple and easy enough for a child to do. They are also intended to be very long term investments – and we typically suggest 18 years – ideally from the day a child is born until you can give them the money at age 18 for them to do as they please!

...and if you don't have children then this works for anyone at any age – as long as you leave it for the long term.

Do we need a broker at this stage?

No we don't. These simple investments into a tracker

fund do not need the intermediary of a broker. When we complete our selection and choice of fund it is very easy to just click through from the comparison website to the fund manager who sells that particular tracker fund and go directly to them without paying any additional or external fees.

In many cases the fund manager will also have an ISA option.

ISA (Individual Savings Account)

If you are a UK resident and tax payer you will have a £20,000 annual ISA allowance (accurate for the 2017-2018 tax year). This means that you can invest up to £20,000 per tax year (6th April in one year to the 5th April the next) and all the income and gains made are tax-free.

It makes sense to use this allowance if you can and in fact, the £20,000 may cover all your investing at Tiers One to Three, making them all tax free.

An ISA is completely flexible and monies can be deposited (up to the annual limit) or withdrawn at any time. With some ISAs the ISA manager decides where to invest the money and in some cases the individual makes those decisions – this is known as a SELF SELECT ISA, which is the one we need for our investing, as we want to make the choices.

No ISA?

If you don't have – or don't want – an ISA then this regular savings approach to the Tier One Cappuccino Strategy works very well in any case.

In other countries or territories there may or may not be a tax-free alternative available to investors – please check your local territory for details.

Ideally, we want to make as much money – and keep as much of it as possible and sometimes the government will help!

Daily Diary

Gill: in my vision of a 'better' world of the future I envisage that every baby will have £/$ 50 per month invested for them from the day they are born. We were able to do it for our children and as a result, our children all have pretty good funds or pensions for the future even though they are still only in their twenties.

With this one simple strategy we could provide a future pension for every child being born today, but it needs a greater level of awareness and co-operation between the parents and the governments.

Small amounts of money turn into huge amounts if they are left long enough. Time is the greatest aid to wealth creation and if we could only start this kind of saving strategy for all children then future generations would not retire in poverty.

Michael: I'm amazed at how easy it is to get started, everyone should know this. It is especially easy when all the investing is done by someone else.

Week Eight: 19th – 25th June 2017

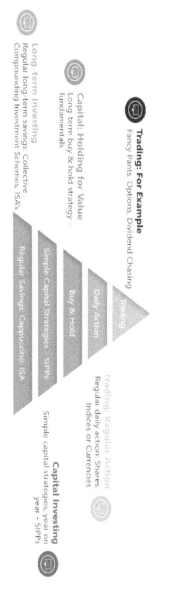

LESSONS and LEARNINGS

Tier One: Summary

Trading: For Example
Fancy Pants, Options, Dividend Chasing

Capital: Holding for Value
Long term buy & hold strategy – fundamentals

Long term Investing
Regular long-term savings: Collective Compounding Investment Schemes, ISA's

Top Level Trading

Trading

Daily Action

Buy & Hold

Simple Capital Strategies - SIPPs

Regular Savings: Cappucino ISA

Trading: Regular Action
Regular daily action: Shares, Indices or Currencies

Capital Investing
Simple capital strategies, year on year - SIPPs

We have now covered all the principles we need to successfully achieve Tier One Investing, and although these principles are all very simple, this is more than most people manage in a lifetime, and yet it's all you need to make a significant difference to your future financial freedom.

The objectives of Tier One are:

1) To get some money put away – on a regular basis – for the future.
2) To leave it accumulating for a long time to allow it to compound and grow.

Plus, as a bonus:

3) To get the income and gains on those savings amount tax-free if we can.

We know that:

We only need to deflect and invest small amounts from our daily expenditure in coffee, magazines, cigarettes or whatever your luxury or wastage might be to make a massive difference to our wealth over time. If we could only see how much those small amounts can accumulate and grow into large amounts, then it would give us the motivation to do without whatever we're spending our money on now. After all, in 30 years' time who is going to remember or care whether we had a special coffee or not – but we WILL care if we have a million in the bank! That's why a compounding calculator works so well –

because it can show us a glimpse of the future money now, and provide the stimulus for action.

Small amounts of savings repeated with regularity also gives us some financial benefits with £/$ cost averaging.

And we also know that:

"Saving is a wonderful thing... especially if your parents do it for you"

Winston Churchill

And there's two benefits that Churchill has identified there: firstly, the starting capital comes from someone else and secondly, your parents are likely to start the savings when you're young – so the money has the potential benefit of the maximum period of time for growth.

But what if your parents couldn't or didn't save for you as soon as you were born?

Well get over it – they were busy! And then get on with it yourself as soon as you can!

Time is vital to this strategy and by delaying by just one year you dramatically reduce the amount you can have at the end of the savings cycle.

Let's just say I am going to save $ 50 per month for 35 years, and I can achieve slightly above our standard and get 11% per annum. With all dividends reinvested, this is how the money compounds over that time:

Compound Investing Chart

Year	Year Deposits	Year Interest	Total Deposits	Total Interest	Balance
1	$600.00	$42.96	$650.00	$42.96	$692.96
2	$600.00	$117.71	$1,250.00	$160.68	$1,410.68
3	$600.00	$201.15	$1,850.00	$361.83	$2,211.83
4	$600.00	$294.30	$2,450.00	$656.13	$3,106.13
5	$600.00	$398.27	$3,050.00	$1,054.39	$4,104.39
6	$600.00	$514.32	$3,650.00	$1,568.72	$5,218.72
7	$600.00	$643.88	$4,250.00	$2,212.59	$6,462.59
8	$600.00	$788.49	$4,850.00	$3,001.08	$7,851.08
9	$600.00	$949.91	$5,450.00	$3,950.99	$9,400.99
10	$600.00	$1,130.10	$6,050.00	$5,081.10	$11,131.10
11	$600.00	$1,331.25	$6,650.00	$6,412.34	$13,062.34
12	$600.00	$1,555.77	$7,250.00	$7,968.12	$15,218.12
13	$600.00	$1,806.40	$7,850.00	$9,774.52	$17,624.52
14	$600.00	$2,086.17	$8,450.00	$11,860.69	$20,310.69
15	$600.00	$2,398.46	$9,050.00	$14,259.15	$23,309.15
16	$600.00	$2,747.06	$9,650.00	$17,006.21	$26,656.21
17	$600.00	$3,136.19	$10,250.00	$20,142.40	$30,392.40
18	$600.00	$3,570.56	$10,850.00	$23,712.95	$34,562.95
19	$600.00	$4,055.42	$11,450.00	$27,768.38	$39,218.38
20	$600.00	$4,596.66	$12,050.00	$32,365.04	$44,415.04
21	$600.00	$5,200.82	$12,650.00	$37,565.86	$50,215.86
22	$600.00	$5,875.22	$13,250.00	$43,441.09	$56,691.09
23	$600.00	$6,628.03	$13,850.00	$50,069.12	$63,919.12
24	$600.00	$7,468.36	$14,450.00	$57,537.48	$71,987.48
25	$600.00	$8,406.38	$15,050.00	$65,943.86	$80,993.86
26	$600.00	$9,453.46	$15,650.00	$75,397.32	$91,047.32
27	$600.00	$10,622.27	$16,250.00	$86,019.59	$102,269.59
28	$600.00	$11,926.97	$16,850.00	$97,946.56	$114,796.56
29	$600.00	$13,383.35	$17,450.00	$111,329.91	$128,779.91
30	$600.00	$15,009.05	$18,050.00	$126,338.95	$144,388.95
31	$600.00	$16,823.75	$18,650.00	$143,162.70	$161,812.70
32	$600.00	$18,849.43	$19,250.00	$162,012.13	$181,262.13
33	$600.00	$21,110.61	$19,850.00	$183,122.73	$202,972.73
34	$600.00	$23,634.67	$20,450.00	$206,757.41	$227,207.41
35	$600.00	$26,452.19	$21,050.00	$233,209.59	$254,259.59

Although the amount of money being invested is the same at $600 per year – the amount of interest increases significantly as time passes: in the first year its only $42.96 but by year 35 it's a staggering $26,452.19.

And of course, if we started just one year later we would lose that future $26k 'benefit'. Now I can do a lot with $26k and I can get that benefit by starting to invest $600 TODAY rather than starting in one year's time. For every year delayed, the amount of lost benefit is significant.

We all know, sadly, how quickly time flies but this is one way we can gain from that passing of time, and the earlier you start the less you need to save overall.

In terms of long-term savings these are the fundamental rules of the game:

Rule One: start as soon as you can

Rule Two: if you're saving for your own future try, as a guide, save at least HALF your age as a % of your annual income. This amount of saving should allow you to live the same kind of lifestyle when you stop work as you did whilst you were working.

If you're 20 now ideally put 10% of your annual income away for the future and if you're 50 now you need to save about 25% of your annual income. As before, the earlier you start the less you have to invest and the cheaper the whole exercise is and trying to start late is difficult – but not impossible.

When you start late, Tier One on its own is not enough to achieve financial security and we have to add other investments to that and consider a slightly different approach which involves a little bit more input in terms of time.

Therefore, we can now start to explore the options in Tier Two where we can invest larger amounts of money in single chunks rather than just small amounts in regular monthly drips.

In return for the larger amounts of money and greater time investment we do however need to obtain a higher rate of return, and set higher targets to achieve.

Let's now look at Tier Two.

Daily Diary

Gill: I constantly get frustrated by most people's attitude to saving and their financial future. Many people want to put it off for later or think that they're too young to start considering the long term - but the reverse is true! You're never too young to start and the earlier you start the greater the gain for the smallest input.

Any future value of money is purely a combination of the return achieved multiplied by the length of time invested. The longer the time the less the return CAN be, and sadly, the shorter the time the higher the return NEEDS to be – and that's when people start taking unnecessary risk. Michael should always be richer than me – eventually – because his wealth accumulation started the day he was born and mine didn't start until I was much older.

Michael: I'm very lucky to have been taught this from a relatively young age. I read about compounding and was taught by my mum, but so few people are that lucky. Most people know they should save money (even if they don't) but very few people know **why** they should. If they did they might be more motivated to.

3. Tier Two

Week Nine: 26th June – 2nd July 2017

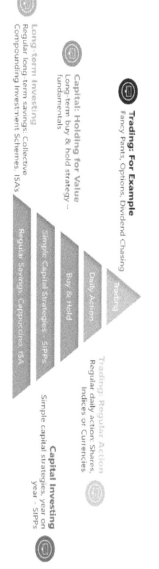

LESSONS and LEARNINGS

Tier Two: moving on!

Top Level Trading

Trading: For Example
Fancy Pants, Options, Dividend Chasing

Capital: Holding for Value
Long-term buy & hold strategy – fundamentals

Long-term Investing
Regular long-term savings: Collective
Compounding Investment Schemes, ISAs

Trading

Daily Action

Buy & Hold

Simple Capital Strategies: SIPPs

Regular Savings: Cappuccino, ISA

Trading: Regular Action
Regular daily action: Shares, Indices or Currencies

Capital Investing
Simple capital strategies, year on year - SIPPs

www.financialinvestingandtrading.com

We now know enough to start investing regular savings into Tier One and leave it for many years and we can move on up to Tier Two.

The aim with Tier Two is to get a higher return than Tier One! In order to get that we need to apply a little bit more brain power and time – but not too much at this stage. We need strategies that fit in Tier Two where we only need input perhaps annually. We need to put in slightly more time and get a slightly better return than Tier One and we can do that by investing in a well-know, tried and tested capital appreciation strategy that is known as the 'Dogs' strategy.

Dogs of the FTSE: Dogs of the DOW

This strategy was originally called the O'Higgins strategy (after the man that first wrote it). Simply, you invest in a very small selection (normally 5 shares and up to a maximum of 10) from a large list of shares (index) like the Dow Jones in America or the FTSE in the UK. When applied, this principle is called the 'Dogs of the Dow', the 'Dogs of the FTSE' or sometimes the 'Beat the FTSE' strategy. It can also be applied to other market indices.

At time of writing the 5 American 'Small Dogs' have generated a 10.4% return per annum between 2000 and 2016. The UK version has generated an average annual 12.2% over the last 15 years. This strategy is only looked at once a year, so is NOT time intensive.

If you want to find out more about the background, then have a look here:
http://www.dogsofthedow.com/

How to find them: FTSE

1) Get a list of the top UK companies – we normally get ours from the Sunday Times where there's a list of the top 200 companies listed in the Business section.

2) Make a list of the top 30 (their rank is written on the furthest left column in the Sunday Times): i.e. the biggest companies and these are the companies with the largest market capitalisation, which is a measure created by multiplying the number of shares in issue times the current market price.

   These are normally listed in any publication just as numbers 1 – 30.

   Make a list of these 30 (We do ours in an Excel spreadsheet so we can repeat often and compare prices) then we sort the data as below.

3) <u>From those 30</u> select the 10 with the **highest** yield. The yield is the amount of income the share generates as a dividend and is included as a separate column in most charts. It is calculated by taking the dividend monetary amount divided by the share price – but for us we don't have to calculate it as it's listed in the paper.

   Then sort those into order so we have the highest 10.

4) <u>From those highest 10</u> then sort by price and select...

5) ...the cheapest 5. And they're the first 5 stock picks!

The cheapest 5 in the list are the 'small dogs' and the other 5 in the list of 10 are the 'larger dogs'.

How to find them: DOW

It is a lot easier to find the 'Dogs of the Dow' because the Dow is already the largest 30 stocks in the US so the first part of the process is already done.

Then download a list of the Dow Jones which is already sorted by yield from:
http://indexarb.com/dividendYieldSorteddj.html

Here's an illustration from that:

The following table is sorted by Dividend Yield.

Stock	Current Price	Estimated Dividend [For the next year]	Dividend Yield (%)
Verizon Communications	45.91	2.3475	5.11
Chevron	106.70	4.3200	4.05
Pfizer	33.92	1.3000	3.83
ExxonMobil	81.65	3.0800	3.77
IBM	160.29	6.0000	3.74
Cisco Systems	34.07	1.1900	3.49
Coca-Cola	43.15	1.5000	3.48
General Electric	28.99	0.9800	3.38
Boeing	184.83	5.8800	3.18
Procter & Gamble	87.33	2.7738	3.18
Merck	62.33	1.9000	3.05
Intel	36.15	1.0900	3.02
Caterpillar	102.26	3.0800	3.01
McDonalds	139.93	3.8600	2.76
Wal Mart	75.18	2.0500	2.73
Johnson & Johnson	123.47	3.3600	2.72
3M	195.83	4.7700	2.44
Microsoft	68.46	1.6400	2.40
Home Depot	156.10	3.7200	2.38
JPMorgan Chase	87.00	2.0600	2.37
Travelers	121.66	2.8800	2.37
United Technologies	118.99	2.7300	2.29
Dupont	79.75	1.5200	1.91
Apple	143.65	2.5200	1.75
American Express	79.25	1.3700	1.73
UnitedHealth Group	174.88	2.9600	1.69
Disney	115.60	1.6300	1.41
NIKE B	55.41	0.7600	1.37
Goldman Sachs	223.80	3.0000	1.34
Visa A	91.22	0.7100	0.78

We then look at only the top ten in the list – i.e. the highest yields and they are our 10 'Dogs' and the cheapest 5 of those are our 'small Dogs'.

And that's it!

My children have been able to identify the 'Dogs' of any stock market index from about the age of 7.

How to do it: any index

1) Now pick a day of the year that is meaningful – either a birthday or anniversary or maybe just the day of the selection process and split whatever money you have available for the process into 5 or 10 pots, depending on how much money you have available to invest and invest in the 5 or 10 'dogs'.

2) Also make sure to invest in the DRIP (Dividend Re Investment Plan) version of the share that automatically reinvest the dividends if available. Your broker should be able to automatically do that for you – or there will be an automatic Reinvestment option when you buy online.

3) Leave those shares invested until the meaningful date one year later, when we do the exercise all over again.

4) If at that time the 5 or 10 shares are the same, leave the selections alone and wait until the meaningful date one year later again, and then repeat, and repeat.

5) If however, when you check after a year, any of the shares are different, sell the share(s) that has dropped off the list and replace it with the share that

has replaced it in the process – and then buy that. If there are two shares that have changed, swap both for the two that have come into the list and so on. Invest ALL the proceeds from the sale of each share in the new one.

For illustration: If a share drops out of the list after one year but has increased in value from £/$ 500 to £/$ 600 use the full £/$600 to go into the replacing share.

Keep repeating this exercise just once a year, year after year, swapping shares in and out as identified until you are ready to sell them all. This is a medium to long-term strategy: say at least 5 – 10 years.

However, it is a successful one! See the results for the 'Dogs of the Dow' below:

WHY does this work?

Investment	Symbol	2012	2013	2014	2015	2016
Dogs of the Dow	-	9.9%	34.9%	10.8%	2.6%	20.1%
Small Dogs of the Dow	-	10.9%	41.2%	14.3%	10.3%	14.1%
Dow Jones Industrials	-	10.2%	29.7%	10.0%	0.2%	16.5%
S&P 500	-	16.0%	32.4%	13.7%	1.4%	12.0%

Investment	1 Year	3 Year	5 Year	10 Year	Since 2000
Dogs of the Dow	20.1%	11.2%	15.7%	9.5%	8.6%
Small Dogs of the Dow	14.1%	12.9%	18.2%	10.0%	10.4%
Dow Jones Industrials	16.5%	8.9%	13.3%	8.9%	6.9%
S&P 500	12.0%	9.0%	15.1%	8.8%	6.2%

The 'Dogs' of the Index is a well established and successful strategy overall because what it is doing is picking well regarded and senior stocks – as they're in the top 30 of the list or Index so they're relatively safe and resilient – but not fail safe, of course!

Then the yield tells us that they are working relatively well as they are paying a dividend (you will have noticed from the list of 30 that some companies are NOT paying dividends and this is usually because they can't afford to) and then added to that they are the cheapest – so they are the value shares in the list.

We know from looking at a very basic share chart that share prices are never flatlining – they are always riding a wave up and down on a daily basis – and what this 'Dogs' technique does is to pick the shares that are at the bottom of their wave rather than the top.

Daily Diary

Gill: I love the 'Dogs' strategy because it makes me feel clever! With such a simple and automated stock selection I can outperform most 'smarty pants' financial experts. I also love the fact that I don't have to think about it – it just IS. The results, over time, speak for themselves. I love it!

Michael: I am really surprised at how simple this strategy is. I like to practice by working out the 'Dogs'. I am also kind of annoyed at how complicated publications and websites make this stuff. It's good to be able to understand business news now.

Week Ten: 3rd – 9th July 2017

LESSONS and LEARNINGS

Tier Two: Dog Investing: How much to invest?

There are three answers to this one so firstly:

How much to invest? Answer One!
Gill's choice

I have to think about how much of my total money that I want to put into each Tier of the Pyramid. I don't want to allocate my money evenly over the Five Tiers as I have a very specific investing strategy and not much of a plan at all at the moment for trading at the top tiers.

Looking at the Pyramid again and each Tier: the regular savings that go into Tier One I can discount as that comes out of my monthly expenses as part of my daily life, so that doesn't need any of my capital.

Then I want to disregard Tiers Four and Five at the moment as I don't know how to do those yet and because I'm older I can't take – and don't want to take – risks. I have decided that when I start trading in the upper Tiers I will paper trade for a while and then work out if I want to allocate funds there. If I think I can trade profitably I can then move a portion of my fund over to a separate account to trade with at a later date.

My overall aim is to invest my money at 10% for 10 years and then withdraw from it for at least the 10 years after that as a pension, and I don't really want anything to interrupt that plan. So if I do actually do any Tier Four and Five trading it's likely to be a smaller thing for me personally. I've decided that at that stage I can just allocate a small amount – maybe £2k – £3k.

At the moment I feel very comfortable with Tiers One and Two and so for now I'm going to allocate all of my available capital funds (roughly £200k) into Tier Two.

I know that I will be making another contribution to that fund in the next year – and for another 9 years after that – so I will always have a bit of new capital arriving that I can use for Tier Three, so for now I'm going to put ALL my capital into Tier Two.

That makes my investing decisions easy and I will just divide that pot of money into 20 chunks and invest in each of the 'Dogs of the Dow' and the 'Dogs of the FTSE' and leave it!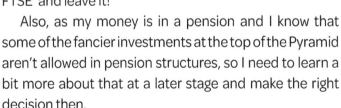

Also, as my money is in a pension and I know that some of the fancier investments at the top of the Pyramid aren't allowed in pension structures, so I need to learn a bit more about that at a later stage and make the right decision then.

Michael's choice
Michael is going to do broadly the same with his Pension

fund money (approximately £35k) and aims to find some cash elsewhere to trade at the higher levels of the Pyramid.

However, Michael is going to only invest in the 'Dogs of the FTSE' at this stage and that's because there is a currency exchange cost of investing in a different currency – dollars in this case – and so he has decided to keep all his money in sterling for now and then learn about currency exchange risk later and then perhaps put his new savings and capital into US stocks later.

Every person would make a slightly different decision at this stage about how to allocate their money, so the things to consider are:

1) What is the overall plan or target?

2) Is the intention to invest and trade on all Five Tiers of the Pyramid and if so what is the timescale for implementing that?

3) Can the Tier One money be allocated out of daily income – and consequently ignored for this exercise?

4) How much capital is available and where is it located? If it's in a pension fund – which has restricted access – then that may restrict choices.

5) Is there likely to be future funds arriving to allocate to different Tiers as knowledge grows?

6) How much 'risk' do you want to take?

7) How much time do you want to allocate to each Tier? A rough rule of thumb is that Tier One needs attention every **18 years** and Tier Five needs **18 minutes** a day.

Use those guiding questions to come up with an initial allocation of funds (we can always change our minds later) and then take whatever portion is available and invest that in Tier Two: 'The Dogs!'

These questions are available as a worksheet and download – click here for access: www.financialinvestingandtrading.com.

How much to invest? Answer Two

Transactions costs and impact on deal sizes

It is clearly vital to keep any transaction fees to an absolute minimum but there's a limit to how low they can go and so those fees have a direct impact on the minimum amounts we should be dealing with.

If we take the 'Dogs of the Dow' strategy as our staple at the moment. We know we can identify them and then trade them execution only with the cheapest broker, but even the cheapest fees will impact the return if the deal size is too small.

Take for instance a deal size of £100. If the transaction charge is £12.95 we can see that 12.95% of our money is immediately lost – so even if the shares return their standard 12% over the year – we will have made no money.

However, that standard £12.95 is only 1.295% if we're investing £1,000 per stock.

If we go back to our basic strategy we can broadly identify a deal size as follows:

1) Identify your target return: our target return is 10% per annum.

2) Identify expected returns: in this case, our evidence tells us that the 'Dogs of the FTSE' make an average of 12.2% and the 'Dogs of the Dow' make 10.4%. For simplicity let's just take an average of those two and say our expected return will be 11.3%.

3) We now know that we have 1.3% available from our projected gain to cover any costs and transaction fees; which is the 11.3% expected return minus target return of 10%.

4) All we need to do now is to work out how much that 'buys us' in terms of deal costs; if our deal cost is £12.95, our minimum deal size needs to be:
£12.95/1.3% all times by 100 = a deal size of £996 per investment.
If, however, our transactions costs **are** only £5, the deal size can be:
£5/1.3% all times by 100 = £384

5) Therefore, get the cheapest quote for a transaction fee as you can and use the formula above to work out your minimum deal size.

6) If we have limited funds it's better to chunk down the investment strategy rather than spreading our investments too thinly and not making money because the charges eat up all the return.

7) This impacts our investment strategy, and if I had restricted amounts of money to invest I would invest as follows:

a) The 5 'small FTSE Dogs' stocks first,
b) Then the 5 'small' Dow stocks second, and
c) Then the second or 'larger' FTSE 5 (shares 6 – 10 on our list),
d) Then the second batch of the Dow stocks.

But some people would invest all their initial funds in their own country and that is great too – so make a decision based on availability of money and where you live!

N.B. if you really don't have enough money to buy the 5 'small Dogs' anywhere then buy just the cheapest one from either list, and then buy the second one next year and so on. It's not ideal but if it gets you going it's worth doing.

How much to invest? Answer Three

As an rough overall guide our minimum needs to be in the range of £400 - £500 per stock purchased, in order for this to make financial sense and for the target return to be achieved. Therefore, on the assumption that we need to invest in at least 5 stocks, as a minimum we need about £/$2,500 capital to get started sensibly on Tier Two.

Daily Diary

Gill: I'm loving how logical and 'formulaic' this is! My one fear at the beginning was that this would take a lot of time and brain power – but so far it's all completely doable with quite small amounts of money and little time!

Michael: This part was always tricky for me, not having access to funds particularly easily but it's encouraging to know that it doesn't matter that much. I am also very confident in the lower tiers especially, to start putting real money into investing.

Week Eleven: 10th – 16th July 2017

LESSONS and LEARNINGS

Tier Two: Dog Investing:

Need to Know!

Although we now know what to invest in there are still some terms to get to grips with before we can actually place the trade with a broker.

a) **Market Capitalisation:** broadly the amount of capital that the company 'represents' in the stock market. This is a general measure of size and is calculated by multiplying the share price by the number of shares in issue. Therefore, as the share price fluctuates, so does the market capitalisation (more commonly known as market cap). The biggest market cap in the UK would be approximately £150 billion, and US companies can be larger in dollar terms, and roughly $200 billion.

   The smallest market cap of a public company would be approximately £150 million, and anything much smaller than that would be listed on a 'grey' market or side market like AIM (Alternative Investment Market).

For the 'Dogs' strategies we deliberately chose from a list of the largest market cap companies, but for other strategies – certainly in Tier Three – we will need this figure as part of our selection criteria.

b) **Yield:** purely the calculation of the income that a share will produce in cash each year, normally in the form of dividends.

The yield is usually expressed as an annual percentage rate based on the investment's cost, but can also be calculated on the current market price. A yield can also be based on historical fact – i.e. past, actually paid dividends or projected future dividends or earnings.

For instance, if we buy a share or stock for $20 and we receive two dividends in the year – one at $1 and one at $1.50 Our total cash income is $2.50 and our yield is:

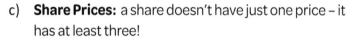

$2.50/$20 * 100 = 12.5%

N.B. 12.5% would be very high for a yield!

c) **Share Prices:** a share doesn't have just one price – it has at least three!

OFFER PRICE This is the price you will pay to buy one share. It is the highest price quoted.

BID PRICE The amount of money you receive when you sell one share. This is the lowest price quoted.

MID PRICE This is the middle of the offer and bid

prices and is used for information only and a share would not be traded at this price. It is normally the price quoted in the newspaper for example and is used as a guide.

N.B. dollars and pence!

Share prices are normally quoted to two decimal places and in the US they are quoted in dollars and cents and in the UK they are normally quoted in PENCE.

If we look at the price of Coca-Cola shares: on the US market they are quoted today at $46.08 and in the UK at 2,360.00. This is in pence so is actually £23.60 and equates fairly accurately to the $46.08 price.

THE SPREAD Is the difference between the bid and offer prices. It is set by a market maker so is more stable.

For large stocks – such as Coca-Cola the spread would be quite narrow – and is in fact only £0.02p on the UK market.

For smaller, less stable companies the spread is likely to be larger.

In the past this spread would be how the brokers made their money – by selling high and buying cheaper – by making a 'turn' on each share.

The spread can vary and it can be wider at some times than others. Normally a

73

spread widens if there is uncertainty (so that the brokers can protect themselves from exposure to price movements).

A spread can also be wider in the morning before the market settles.

HIGH AND LOW Bid and Offer prices are not often clearly apparent when looking at share price lists – and they are not to be confused with the high and low price which is generally very clearly noted.

The high and low price are the peak and trough of a share price over the time period being reviewed; so in most cases it will be the highest price achieved by the share – and then the lowest price achieved – during a trading day.

However, if you are looking at, say, a six month chart or annual figures, the high and low prices will be the highest and lowest over the six months or year being reviewed.

You can review the high and low prices over very short time periods, like an hour, and these are normally presented in charts. Although that level of detail isn't needed for Tier Two investments they are useful for trading at Tiers Four and Five.

d) **The Market Maker:** The market maker is the broker organisation that sets the share prices. Normally a market maker sets the price for specific stocks and in the UK, for instance, there has to be at least TWO market makers per stock or share operating at all times. What this means is that a person who wants to invest or trade can always do that because there is a market maker who has to pick up the other side of the transaction. Market makers normally hold large quantities of the stock they set the price for so they can ALWAYS deal.

The general public gets access to market makers through normal public brokers (which we will cover in another chapter) although some market makers do deal with the general public as well.

The New York Stock Exchange (NYSE) has Designated Market Makers, formerly known as "specialists", who act as the official market maker for a given security. Other US  exchanges, most prominently the NASDAQ Stock Exchange, employ several competing official market makers in a security.

The market makers do not really have any impact or interaction with individuals who want to trade but it's good to know that there will always be someone picking up whatever trades we want to do!

e) **Placing an order**

Buying at 'market' means you get the share price of the exchange when the order is placed (which is generally automatic).

Buying at 'limit' is setting a price you want specifically so, your order may not get filled if the price doesn't reach the price you have specified, and will naturally 'expire'.

As a general rule, trade with limit orders when the deal is price sensitive for the strategy you're trading and this would be some of the strategies at Tiers Four and Five such as channelling.

For Tier One to Three investing the price isn't that important to the strategy as they are long-term strategies, so market orders are fine.

Daily Diary

Gill: Eventually the regulators will simplify pricing but for now we have to put up with the many different prices per day on the same shares!

Michael: It took some time to get used to the broker user interface and every broker is different. A good thing to do is get a demo account (most provide this) and mess around putting on fake trades.

Week Twelve: 17th – 23rd July 2017

LESSONS and LEARNINGS

Tier Two: Dog Investing:

Need to Know: Part TWO!

Dividends

So far, we've only looked at capital appreciation strategies, and it's worth clarifying the differences between income generation and capital appreciation before we make any real investments.

The income from a share comes in the form of dividends, which are the payments that a business makes out of annual profits to the owners of the business. If we owned a private business just as an individual, we would be entitled to receive the entire profits of a business – with certain restrictions and tax charges, of course!

With a larger public company that profit is distributed back to the owners, or shareholders, as income or dividends. There are normally two dividends per year – an interim payment and then a final annual payment. Dividends are normally expressed in pence or cents per share.

If you own 100 shares and there is a dividend payment of 5 cents or pence per share you will receive £/$5 as a dividend payment. Dividends are normally paid in cash – although there are some cases where these dividends are "paid" in additional shares.

A dividend is paid out of profits after all other expenses – and so if there's no money left over after paying everything else then the company won't be able to pay a dividend at all.

There are three dates to note when receiving dividends.

The people who own the shares at the ex dividend (Ex D) date, are then entitled to receive the dividend when it is paid. The Ex D date is about 2 weeks before the exact dividend is confirmed or declared – and then the dividend pay date is some time after that. The Ex D date is important as a share price will move up in expectation of a dividend being declared – and just before the Ex D date.

There is an income strategy where you buy a share just before the Ex D – getting the entitlement to the dividend and then selling the share the day after – before the dividend was declared or paid. The dividend is always paid to the person who owns the shares on the Ex D date and so you could have sold the shares long before the dividend was actually paid and still get the dividend. The income strategy then is to buy a share just before Ex D date and then sell again immediately – but as a share price often moves up in anticipation of a dividend the gain can be quite small.

Capital versus income

These dividends equate to the interest received on a bank deposit, for instance. With a bank deposit the principle amount is more or less guaranteed and the interest received is predetermined – and will be tied to, in the main, the countries base rate.

With a bank deposit we get the certainty of the interest to come and the comfort of the safety of the principle deposited, but the interest paid will be small – say less than 1% per annum.

With a share our stake, or "deposit", is not guaranteed but the dividends tend to be slightly larger – certainly on mainstream stocks and shares.

Tiers One and Two

However, with the strategies in Tiers One and Two of our Pyramid we generally don't want the dividend!

The returns we want to get at around 10% will only be achieved if we reinvest all the dividends immediately, and we need to make sure that we don't actually get any of those dividends in cash and make sure they are immediately re-invested. There are a few ways to do that:

1) Accumulation Units. In the Tier One tracker fund investment we specifically looked for accumulation units or accumulation shares rather than income ones.

The accumulation unit automatically accumulates all the dividends into the pot of shares and doesn't distribute or pay them out. The share or unit price will move up as a result of a dividend because the pot of money overall has increased.

2) With a share it is slightly more complicated and there are two ways to make sure the dividend gets reinvested:

a) Buy DRIP shares. A DRIP (Dividend Reinvestment Plan) share is one where the company pays the dividend, not in cash as normal, but in the allocation of more shares – and even part shares, so the dividend is automatically and immediately 'reinvested' as another share. There is no broker commission to be paid on this either – so there is a double benefit. It is worth checking BEFORE you buy any share if they have a DRIP share option so that you get the right share – and your broker will help with that.

b) For some companies – and some brokers – there is no DRIP option but you should still be able to state in your share trading, broker account that you want all dividends reinvested. There will normally be a limit you can set to say that all dividends over £1 or £10 or whatever are to be reinvested – check your own broker account for their limits. There will normally be a broker fee for that transaction.

Illustration

Here is a screen shot from my broker account and it tells me that I have selected automatic dividend reinvestment as a default option and then it lists the shares that have the DRIP shares available.

portfolio > dividend reinvestment

dividend reinvestment | 0926304 - Pension Trading Account

On this page you can choose to automatically reinvest Sterling dividends into the stocks they are received on.

- Dividend reinvestment is available for popular shares (including the FTSE 350) and a range of Investment Trusts and ETFs.
- The Dividend must be paid onto your account in sterling for it to be reinvested.
- If you elect for Dividend Reinvestment, this will take place usually within two Business Days following payment of the dividend to your account.
- Once a reinvestment is complete, you will receive a contract note confirming the reinvestment has taken place.
- In order for the dividend to be reinvested it should have a value of £10 or more.
- If you sell or transfer out your entire holding in a stock before the dividend is reinvested then the reinvestment will not take place.
- If there is a Corporate Action on a stock, your dividend preference may be removed. If this happens you will need to reset your preference.
- A charge will be levied for each Dividend Reinvestment, please see the rates and charges for details.

dividend reinvestment

Default Preference

Always select Dividend Reinvestment for any purchases or deposits of Stock that are eligible in this account   ✓   Save Changes

Eligible Stocks in my Portfolio

Symbol	Quantity Held	Description	
AZN	221	ASTRAZENEPAR	✓
BP.	2,318	BPPAR	✓
BT.A	3,374	BT GROUPAR	✓
GSK	663	GLAXOSMITPAR	✓
HSBA	1,360	HSBC HLDGPAR	✓
IMB	292	IMPL BRANPAR	✓
NG.	1,061	NATL GRIDPAR	✓
RDSB	481	ROYAL DUT'B'	✓
RDSA	471	ROYAL DUTCH'A'	✓
VOD	4,522	VODE GROU	✓

Summary

We are now ready to invest in our Tier Two choices – the 'Dogs' strategy. This is a capital strategy – we want all capital and income to keep rolling up in order to achieve that 10%.

We also need a broker account through which we can buy and sell our shares.

Daily Diary

Gill: I love the accumulation principle and the fact that I can get income on my income and watch the money compound up over time! I have no need at the moment for any income as I'm still working and earning – so for now I can watch my money grow towards my target.

Michael: With the amount of return I know that these low Tier strategies can provide, it won't let me quit my day job but an easy pension is nothing to complain about and something I know a lot of people my age worry about. I read about compounding not too long ago and I am still amazed how much of a difference it makes when investing.

Week Thirteen: 24th – 30th July 2017

LESSONS and LEARNINGS

Tier Two: Dog Investing

How to do it

Identifying which shares fall into the category of the 'Dogs' criteria is relatively easy once you get used to the process, but if you've never invested before what you do and how you do it can be daunting at first.

The Tier One investments – the collective investment/ mutual funds – can be made directly with the fund manager but with Tier Two investments, and in order to invest in these 'Dogs' anywhere in the world, we need a broker.

A broker is purely an intermediary that has access to the relevant stock exchanges as it isn't possible for a normal human to go direct to the stock exchange itself.

FINDING A BROKER

I've now discovered that finding a broker is quite challenging as there are so many and their services and fees aren't always transparent!

Starting from the top I know I need to look at:

1) The type of broker service. Brokers are in three camps:

   - Execution only – these brokers act on my instructions and I am totally in control as the decision maker. These brokers only do what I ask them to do, and these are the cheapest as, in general, they can be easily accessed online, and you don't actually get to see a human.

   - Advisory – where the broker gives you advice on what to buy and sell; they do certain amounts of research and make recommendations which you either accept or not. These brokers would probably meet you in person and charge a medium level of fee, and

   - Discretionary – where you hand over your investment money to a broker who decides what to do buy and sell and they do everything for you. In this case the broker makes all the decisions and has all the control. This is very expensive and tends to be only for people with very large portfolios, and lots of money!

At the beginning we are going to be picking shares from simple predetermined strategies so all we need at the moment is a basic, cheap execution-only broker that we can use to trade online.

2) I would prefer to use a broker that is regulated to provide financial services. In the UK this would be FCA (Financial Conduct Authority) registered, in the USA the lead regulatory body is the SEC (Securities Exchange Commission) – although in the USA there are many specific federal bodies plus State specific banking regulations – and in Australia for instance it would be APRA (Australian Prudential Regulatory Authority).

   Ensuring that your broker is regulated gives a certain degree of protection because you know they are independently monitored and they comply with basic money legislations.

3) The broker we choose needs to be able to transact the types of trading and investing we want to do. This should be relatively easy for the bottom three Tiers of the Pyramid: i.e. the investing strategies should be provided by most if not all brokers. However, not all brokers offer the services to enable us to trade at the Tiers Four or Five of the Pyramid such as daily trades or with options, for instance.

   It may be necessary to have different brokers for the top two Tiers of our Pyramid but for now we just need to find one that will be able to transact the simple stuff.

www.financialinvestingandtrading.com

4) For Michael and I specifically, because we are investing monies in a pension environment, we also have to find a broker that is approved and used by that pensions manager – even though we have complete choice for where the money is invested.

   N.B. if you are doing something similar and investing through another environment such as a pension or an ISA or similar you probably need to find the fund provider FIRST and then use a broker from their accepted or recommended list.

5) Best price: The first thing I notice about the broker list is that they all tend to offer two prices for transacting trades: a frequent trader price and a normal price. Now at this stage in our learning and trading we are NOT going to be frequent traders as the intention initially is to do 12 trades in one year.

   The charge is per transaction so if we buy the 5 small 'Dogs of the Dow' for instance that will be 5 separate trades.

   The transaction fees range from about £5 per frequent trade to £12.50 for a normal trade, so in any case the fees are relatively small – but may have an impact on smaller investments! Curiously, the rate is about the same in the USA ranging from about $5 to $15

   Many brokers will offer discounts and 'free' trades to get you signed up with them, so shop around for one that works for you.

   As a guide, if you are doing investing in Tiers One to Three then you're likely to do about 20 trades per year – so however you look at it this we are INfrequent traders, in general terms.

6) Familiarity: Looking down the list of potential brokers I can see that most of the 'high street' banks in the UK offer share dealing services and if you have a strong relationship with your particular bank that might be an option for you.

There is another that offers 'online social dealing' which I'm not interested in as I don't 'do' social media very well – but you might!

7) Percentage trade deals: There are a couple of brokers that charge a percentage of your trade – for instance 1% per trade and we certainly don't want that as our actual transaction amount is going to be fairly small. These brokers might work out cheaper for you if your average deal size was up to about £1,000. Anything over that and it's probably cheaper to get a fixed transaction price. For instance, if your transaction amount is going to be £5,000 then paying 1% as a transaction fee would be £50, rather than say £10 as a fixed price fee.

8) Global involvement: If you're likely to be trading or investing across the globe it might be worth looking at a broker that has offices in all territories and the most likely one of those is the TD/ii group. Interactive Investor (ii) has just taken over a large part of TD so that is likely to be the biggest global broker presence for our needs.

Finally, as the list of potential brokers that fit all those criteria is likely to be reasonably short (just put the list into a search engine on the computer), visit each of their websites and have a flick and click around and see what one suits you best – and pick that one!

Daily Diary

Gill: I've been surprised how easy it has been to choose a broker – they all seem customer friendly and all have easy training type guides on their websites. I've also called a few of the call centres and whilst they may not be ideal information providers – they can help and direct if you get stuck.

Michael: All brokers provide different services so it would seem there is a broker for everyone. When comparing brokers there is a lot of information that can be found from a quick online search. Don't forget calling up helplines or emailing them is an easy way of finding if a broker will work for you as they are usually quite helpful.

Week Fourteen: 31st July – 6th August 2017

LESSONS and LEARNINGS

Tier Two: Dog Investing

How to do it: Opening a trading account

Once we have chosen our broker then all we need to do is to open an account. It doesn't matter where you live or what you intend to trade as most larger brokers – like the global ii group we have already identified – will trade anything and anywhere and will guide you through the different practices for different countries and assets as you go.

All the larger brokers will also allow you to open a 'research' or 'dummy' (sometimes called paper trading) account to practice with first, which can then be converted into a real account that you can load money into and then use as normal. It makes sense to start with a research type of account until you get used to the processing – although all are fairly intuitive and relatively easy to operate – and all the major brokers have a help desk and or a chat room facility that can help you through any issue.

It also makes sense to open two research accounts

– with different brokers – to practice with, as one will inevitably suit you better than another – so find the one you like best and that will help with the investing. Having two accounts also gives you some flexibility and choice later on – if one is doing a special offer on transaction fees, for instance.

Just log onto your broker of choice and follow the menus!

For illustration purposes here are two or the larger brokers: interactive investor (ii) and TD Ameritrade.

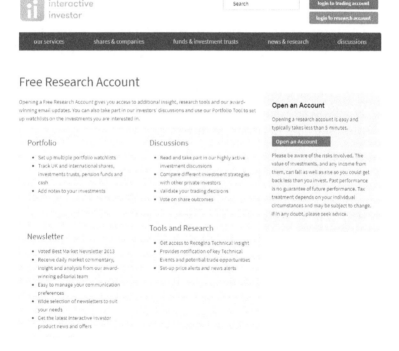

Interactive Investor (UK Based)

If you click on the 'open an account' button you will then have to:

1) Create a password and username
2) Put in your name and address
3) Select what newsletters you want to receive,
4) Click on contact options and the terms and conditions,
5) Click on submit – and that's it!

You will probably receive a conformation e-mail before you can click on and off and there you are – account opened.

When you are ready to trade with real money you can then convert your research account into a live account – and at that stage you will have to provide proof of identity and upload a couple of pieces of evidence (passport, or driving license and a utility bill for example). Of course, we need to add some money!

TD Ameritrade (USA, plus Canada, Singapore and Malaysia)

If we click on the Open New Account Button we get taken to a similar account opening page, which also has links to opening accounts for people based in Canada, Singapore, and Malaysia.

Ameritrade (1) 2 3 4 5

Start Your Application

Need help? Call us.
800-454-9272
[-] Leave feedback

It's easy.

Open an account in five simple steps.

Welcome! You'll soon have access to an array of investment products, trading tools, and educational resources—all with straightforward pricing and no hidden fees.

What you'll need to open an account:

- A few minutes to complete this form
- Social Security Number (SSN) or Individual Taxpayer Identification Number (ITIN)
- Foreign tax ID, passport, or visa number (if you're not a citizen or permanent resident of the U.S.)
- Employer's name and address

Note: If you are a resident of Canada, Singapore, or Malaysia, visit these sites to open your account

Do you already have an account with us?

This includes a paperMoney® account.

○ Yes, please prefill parts of my application.

● No, I'm a new client.

Your contact information

Prefix (optional)

Select ⌄

First name

Middle name (optional)

The information is very similar to that needed for the interactive investor account, although the distinction between research account and trading account isn't the same.

However, the research facilities are also provided:

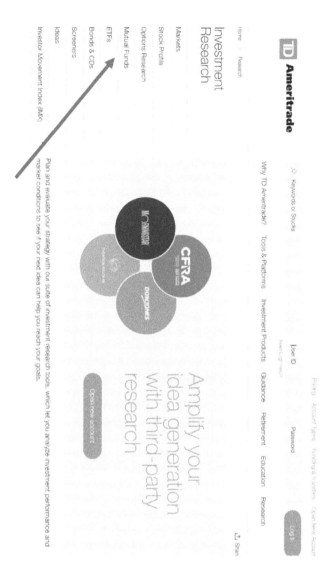

N.B. this research area of the TD Ameritrade account will also give you the information on Mutual Funds and EFTs that we need for the Cappuccino factor fund selection in Tier One of the Pyramid.

Investing in Different Countries

When investing in different territories to the one you reside in, the broker system should ask you for more information.

For example, when trying to invest in US (International) stocks from the UK we get presented with this message:

Place An Order

| Investment type | UK Shares & ETFs | Funds | **International** | Bonds & Warrants |

| Account Number | 0926304 - Pension Trading Account ▾ |

⚠ To trade and get quotes for non-UK stocks you first need to sign the exchange agreements

All you have to do is to click on the link and complete the 'exchange agreement' which also then linked me through to completing the W8 – BEN which is a form for the US tax authorities for identification.

Useful Forms

We have provided a range of online and PDF forms which you'll find helpful when managing your account.

Form Type:

United States Dealing ▾

As part of our obligations to the US Tax Authorities - Internal Revenue Service (IRS) we are required to document all holders of US securities. Additionally, should you reside in a country that has a treaty with the US you may benefit from treaty relief in respect of dividend and interest payments. If you wish to invest in US (United States) stocks and shares, you will need to complete the appropriate form W-8, depending on your account type.

Please note: On selecting this for the first time you will be presented with an error screen. Please return in 15 minutes where your account will be updated and the W8BEN can be completed.

For further information and official guidance please visit the IRS.gov website.

❶ Joint Trading Accounts

Complete this form per joint holder.

Please ensure you read the W-8BEN guidance notes prior to completion.

🗔 **W-8BEN Form**

🗔 View   ⬇ Download

🗔 **W-8BEN guidance notes**

🗔 View   ⬇ Download

DO NOT WORRY about these forms before you start!

As you go through each broker's account they will stop you, when needed to, complete different pages for different countries. All of them are self explanatory and their help desk will guide you, if needed.

Only complete each form as you need it and you will need to complete a form for each separate broker – but once you've done it once you can just copy the details each time.

IF you hit a form that needs to be completed it may slow you down a day or two with your investing whilst the details are confirmed, but then you'll be up and running, and this is far preferable than trying to l every form that you think you may need in the future ahead of any real investing.

You will **NOT** need to open an account in different territories for shares in different countries – your homebased broker will be able to transact all the shares we look at in the bottom three Tiers of our Pyramid. Therefore, the order of broker accounts should be:

1) Research or paper or dummy before real,
2) Home territory before overseas

How long to Paper Trade?

NOT LONG!

Some people suggest that you should paper trade for long periods of time when you first start investing and I may agree with that IF we were doing day trading (Tiers Four or Five of the Pyramid) but at this stage we are only investing in tried and tested strategies. Whilst it is useful to paper trade just once or twice to see HOW the order process works and so on, there is no benefit in paper trading at the bottom Two Tiers of the Pyramid – in fact, it will diminish your returns because TIME is of the essence with the first strategies; the regular savings 'Cappuccino' factor approach and the 'Dogs' strategy.

Later on, and with the more sophisticated strategies of say forex and commodity trading, there is more sense in paper trading as this enables you to practice placing and exiting the deals without losing any real money.

However, there is no learning experience like the one where you gain or lose real money so I'm not a fan of paper trading for too long, as paper traders have a habit of saying they **would** have done such and such, whereas in real time and with real money – they wouldn't!

As long as you control your risk and understand what the deals are about then I wouldn't paper trade for more than a month or two before I wanted to jump in and see how it really feels to go live.

But that's for much later in our journey and for now we don't really need to paper trade, other than to test which buttons to press when investing in the shares we want.

Daily Diary

Gill: I now have my broker account open – for UK and US stocks. I have my money ready and I understand the 'Dogs' strategy – all I need to do now is to PLACE those trades!

Michael: It took a while to get my account running as I had to open it through my pension account. I would encourage people to stick with it so you can start investing as quickly as possible.

Week Fifteen: 7th – 13th August 2017

LESSONS and LEARNINGS

Tier Two: Dog Investing

Taking action: PLACE those trades!

Gill's Choice

My plan is to take my money and divide it into 10 pots of £10k for the UK and then 10 pots of £9,750 for the US 'Dogs' stocks, to total my £197,825 (more or less).

I have now quickly redone my 'Dogs' Strategy to see what trades I need to place today and I've come up with a list:

UK DOGS OF THE FTSE (end of July 2017)

Vodafone
BT
HSBC
Astra Zeneca
Glaxo Smith Kline
Royal Dutch Shell 'A'
Royal Dutch Shell 'B'

Imperial Brands
National Grid
BP

And I just clicked on my account and started placing the orders!

N.B. Trading size: what I did was just order £10k of each stock at market price and the computer then worked out how many to buy. I wanted my £10k to include all dealing costs and stamp duty in each case – so I've now got slightly less than £10k of the shares but all fees have been paid.

The starting Position

The trades themselves

Order Confirmation

✓ Thank you. Your order is confirmed

Order ref:	KFRWQ2
Buying	4,522 VODAFONE GROUP ORD USD0.2095238 (VOD)
Status:	Executed
Placed at:	11:44:15 28/07/17
Price:	£2.198755
Order Type:	Market
✓ TD DIRECT INVESTING PRICE IMPROVEMENT	TD Direct Investing improved your order by £3.37

Order Confirmation

✓ Thank you. Your order is confirmed

Order ref:	KFRWSC
Buying	3,256 BT GROUP ORD GBP0.05 (BT.A)
Status:	Executed
Placed at:	11:46:35 28/07/17
Price:	£3.0539
Order Type:	Market
✓ TD DIRECT INVESTING PRICE IMPROVEMENT	TD Direct Investing improved your order by £0.33

Order Confirmation

✓ Thank you. Your order is confirmed

Order ref:	KFRWVK
Buying	1,334 HSBC HOLDINGS PLC ORD USD0.50 (HSBA)
Status:	Executed
Placed at:	11:50:16 28/07/17
Price:	£7.451505
Order Type:	Market
✓ TD DIRECT INVESTING PRICE IMPROVEMENT	TD Direct Investing improved your order by £0.66

Order Confirmation

✓ Thank you. Your order is confirmed

Order ref:	KFRWZM
Buying	655 GLAXOSMITHKLINE ORD GBP0.25 (GSK)
Status:	Executed
Placed at:	11:56:14 28/07/17
Price:	£15.1676
Order Type:	Market
✓ TD DIRECT INVESTING PRICE IMPROVEMENT	TD Direct Investing improved your order by £1.57

Order Confirmation

✅ Thank you. Your order has been received and we will attempt to execute your instruction as soon as possible

Order ref:	**KFRW4F**
Buying	**£10,000.00 ROYAL DUTCH SHELL 'A'SHS EUR0.07(GBP) (RDSA)**
Status:	**Pending**
Placed at:	**12:00:47 28/07/17**
Order Type:	**Market Best**

Order Confirmation

✅ Thank you. Your order is confirmed

Order ref:	**KFRW5G**
Buying	**468 ROYAL DUTCH SHELL 'B'ORD EUR0.07 (RDSB)**
Status:	**Executed**
Placed at:	**12:03:14 28/07/17**
Price:	**£21.2151**
Order Type:	**Market**
✅ **TD DIRECT INVESTING PRICE IMPROVEMENT**	TD Direct Investing improved your order by **£2.29**

Order Confirmation

✅ Thank you. Your order is confirmed

Order ref:	**KFRW6F**
Buying	**290 IMPERIAL BRANDS PLC GBP0.10 (IMB)**
Status:	**Executed**
Placed at:	**12:05:20 28/07/17**
Price:	**£34.1951**
Order Type:	**Market**
✅ **TD DIRECT INVESTING PRICE IMPROVEMENT**	TD Direct Investing improved your order by **£1.42**

However there were three of the ten 'DOGS' stocks that didn't go through immediately: two (BP and National Grid) showed as 'failed' on my order sheet (see below).

I phoned the trading desk to see why that was and apparently the price was moving too quickly to get a firm deal price – so they said just retry and I did and it worked.

However they did say that if that happens again just to call in just in case the order is placed in pending or somewhere and I end up doing the order twice – so watch out for that one.

The final stock of the Ten for me was Astra Zeneca and when I looked at it the price was so different to what was quoted in the Sunday Times the previous week that I checked the share on the internet to see that the price had plummeted. That doesn't bother me per se but it may distort its position in the 10 'Dogs' stocks as the falling share price may mean that the yield is not now in the range for the stock to qualify under this particular strategy.

Therefore, I rechecked the Astra Zeneca share and it still came within the 'Dogs' selection so I just went back in and did it the next day.

The order list showing the 'failed' trades

Description	Quantity	Expiry Date	Settlement Date	Total	Status
VODAFONE GROUP ORD USD0.2095238	4,522	n/a	01/08/17	£9,998.43	Executed
BT GROUP ORD GBP0.05	3,256	n/a	01/08/17	£9,999.17	Executed
BP ORD USD0.25	2,247	n/a	n/a	£9,998.08	Failed
HSBC HOLDINGS PLC ORD USD0.50	1,334	n/a	01/08/17	£9,995.06	Executed
NATIONAL GRID ORD GBP0.12431289	1,060	n/a	n/a	£9,991.03	Failed
GLAXOSMITHKLINE ORD GBP0.25	655	n/a	01/08/17	£9,990.40	Executed
ROYAL DUTCH SHELL 'A'SHS EUR0.07(GBP)	£10,000	n/a	01/08/17	£9,980.75	Executed
ROYAL DUTCH SHELL 'B'ORD EUR0.07	468	n/a	01/08/17	£9,984.26	Executed
IMPERIAL BRANDS PLC GBP0.10	290	n/a	01/08/17	£9,972.11	Executed

The two failed trades re-ordered

Order Confirmation

✓ Thank you. Your order is confirmed

Order ref:	KFRXVX
Buying	1,061 NATIONAL GRID ORD GBP0.12431289 (NG.)
Status:	Executed
Placed at:	12:48:59 28/07/17
Price:	£9.37002
Order Type:	Market
✓ TD DIRECT INVESTING PRICE IMPROVEMENT	TD Direct Investing improved your order by £1.04

Order Confirmation

✓ Thank you. Your order is confirmed

Order ref:	KFRXWJ
Buying	2,251 BP ORD USD0.25 (BP.)
Status:	Executed
Placed at:	12:50:22 28/07/17
Price:	£4.41701
Order Type:	Market
✓ TD DIRECT INVESTING PRICE IMPROVEMENT	TD Direct Investing improved your order by £1.10

The 'final' portfolio of Nine stocks – with the Astra Zeneca missing – for the moment.

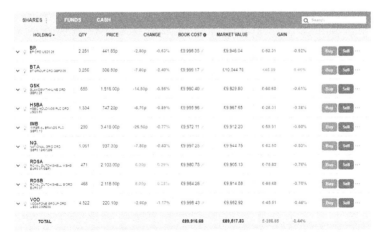

HOLDING ▼	QTY	PRICE	CHANGE		BOOK COST	MARKET VALUE	GAIN			
BP. BP ORD USD0.25	2,251	441.85p	-2.80p	-0.63%	£9,998.35	£9,946.04	£-52.31	-0.52%	Buy Sell	
BT.A BT GROUP ORD GBP0.05	3,256	308.50p	-7.80p	-2.46%	£9,999.17	£10,044.76	£45.59	0.46%	Buy Sell	
GSK GLAXOSMITHKLINE ORD GBP0.25	655	1,516.00p	-14.50p	-0.86%	£9,990.40	£9,929.80	£-60.60	-0.61%	Buy Sell	
HSBA HSBC HOLDINGS PLC ORD USD0.50	1,334	747.20p	-6.70p	-0.89%	£9,995.96	£9,967.65	£-28.31	-0.28%	Buy Sell	
IMB IMPERIAL BRANDS PLC GBP0.10	290	3,418.00p	-26.50p	-0.77%	£9,972.11	£9,912.20	£-59.91	-0.60%	Buy Sell	
NG. NATIONAL GRID ORD GBP0.12431289	1,061	937.30p	-7.80p	-0.83%	£9,997.25	£9,944.75	£-52.50	-0.53%	Buy Sell	
RDSA ROYAL DUTCH SHELL 'A'SHS EUR0.07(GBP)	471	2,103.00p	6.00p	0.29%	£9,980.75	£9,905.13	£-75.62	-0.76%	Buy Sell	
RDSB ROYAL DUTCH SHELL B ORD EUR0.07	468	2,118.50p	8.00p	0.38%	£9,984.26	£9,914.58	£-69.68	-0.70%	Buy Sell	
VOD VODAFONE GROUP ORD USD0.20952	4,522	220.10p	-2.60p	-1.17%	£9,998.43	£9,952.92	£-45.51	-0.46%	Buy Sell	
TOTAL					£89,916.68	£89,517.83	£-398.85	-0.44%		

And the final stock purchased!

Order Confirmation

⊘ Thank you. Your order is confirmed

Order ref:	**KFSGQ2**
Buying	**218 ASTRAZENECA ORD USD0.25 (AZN)**
Status:	**Executed**
Placed at:	**09:54:39 31/07/17**
Price:	**£45.5417**
Order Type:	**Market**
⊘ TD DIRECT INVESTING PRICE IMPROVEMENT	TD Direct Investing improved your order by **£0.72**

DOGS OF THE DOW

I then moved onto checking the 'Dogs of the Dow' and I was able to identify the 10 stocks pretty quickly from the yield list:

The following table is sorted by Dividend Yield.

Stock	Current Price	Estimated Dividend [For the next year]	Dividend Yield (%)	Bar Graph
Verizon Communications	47.81	2.3600	4.94	
IBM	145.07	6.1000	4.20	
Chevron	106.11	4.3200	4.07	
Pfizer	33.00	1.3200	4.00	
Cisco Systems	31.57	1.2200	3.86	
General Electric	25.79	0.9900	3.84	
ExxonMobil	80.83	3.1000	3.84	
Coca-Cola	46.12	1.5200	3.30	
Intel	34.97	1.1075	3.17	
Procter & Gamble	90.68	2.7892	3.08	

I got stumped on the trading temporarily as I needed to complete my disclosure agreement and the W8BEN form which I did.

Place An Order

| Investment type | UK Shares & ETFs | Funds | International | Bonds & Warrants |

| Account Number | 0926304 - Pension Trading Account ▼ |

To trade and get quotes for non-UK stocks you first need to sign the exchange agreements

And then I had to do the W8BEN

Useful Forms

We have provided a range of online and PDF forms which you'll find helpful when managing your account.

Form Type: United States Dealing ▼

As part of our obligations to the US Tax Authorities - Internal Revenue Service (IRS) we are required to document all holders of US securities. Additionally, should you reside in a country that has a treaty with the US you may benefit from treaty relief in respect of dividend and interest payments. If you wish to invest in US (United States) stocks and shares, you will need to complete the appropriate form W-8, depending on your account type.

Please note: On selecting this for the first time you will be presented with an error screen. Please return in 15 minutes where your account will be updated and the W8BEN can be completed.

For further information and official guidance please visit the IRS.gov website.

❶ Joint Trading Accounts

Complete this form per joint holder.

Please ensure you read the W-8BEN guidance notes prior to completion.

W-8BEN Form
View   Download

W-8BEN guidance notes
View   Download

107

www.financialinvestingandtrading.com

N.B. As I'm investing via my pension I needed to do (or at least my SIPP company has to do) a different specialist form – so you may need to get help from your pension provider etc if you are investing in the same way as we are – if not, a standard W8 BEN form is fine.

If I were investing as an individual this bit would be easy!

This caused me a delay of a few weeks sadly but eventually I got my US 'Dogs of the Dow' invested:

Symbol	Buy/Sell	Links	Qty	Description	Price	Price Change $	Price Change %	Market Value	Book Cost	Gain / Loss $	Gain / Loss %
CVX	Buy Sell		115	CHEVRON CORPORATION COM USD0.75	$111.10	$1.67	1.52%	$12,776.50	$12,514.03	$262.47	2.10%
CSCO	Buy Sell		390	CISCO SYSTEMS INC COM USD0.001	$31.67	$0.055	0.17%	$12,351.30	$12,468.28	$-116.98	-0.94%
KO	Buy Sell		265	COCA-COLA CO COM USD0.25	$45.97	$0.055	0.12%	$12,182.05	$12,144.50	$37.55	0.31%
XOM	Buy Sell		160	EXXON MOBIL CORPORATION COM NPV	$78.51	$1.34	1.73%	$12,561.60	$12,498.98	$62.62	0.50%
GE	Buy Sell		495	GENERAL ELECTRIC CO COM USD0.06	$24.93	$0.17	0.69%	$12,340.35	$12,491.68	$-151.33	-1.21%
INTC	Buy Sell		345	INTEL CORP COM USD0.001	$35.67	$0.66	1.88%	$12,306.15	$12,531.28	$-225.13	-1.80%
IBM	Buy Sell		90	INTERNATIONAL BUS MACH CORP COM USD0.20	$144.27	$1.25	0.87%	$12,984.30	$12,837.28	$147.02	1.15%
MRK	Buy Sell		200	MERCK & CO INC COM USD0.50	$64.04	$0.42	0.66%	$12,808.00	$12,541.78	$266.22	2.12%
PFE	Buy Sell		375	PFIZER INC COM USD0.05	$33.96	$0.16	0.47%	$12,735.00	$12,510.28	$224.72	1.90%
VZ	Buy Sell		255	VERIZON COMMUNICATIONS COM USD0.10	$47.25	$-0.11	-0.23%	$12,048.75	$12,393.13	$-344.38	-2.78%
								$125,094.00	$124,931.22	$162.78	0.13%

Now in theory I can stop for a year and not do anything – but I suspect I will take a peek at the portfolio from time to time – not to change them but to see how they're doing.

History tells me that the shares selected from the 'Dogs of the FTSE' or the 'Dogs of the Dow' have generated over time, somewhere between 11% - 14% per annum, and that's easily going to enable me to reach my 10% target return.

In fact, all I need is a rise of about 0.83% per month and I'm on track for the year. I doubt very much whether the growth will be as steady and consistent as that but 0.83% seems a very small amount and achievable.

Daily Diary

Gill: There were times when that felt a bit tortuous and I was unsure when, for instance, the deals failed as to what to do – but I just phoned the broker up and got it sorted – so all ended up fine, and I now know what to do if that situation occurs again – and next time I will click and flick about like an experienced trader!

It was also frustrating to have to wait for my pension provider to complete the W8Ben when I could have done a personal form in the blink of an eye – but hey ho – it still all worked out OK in the end.

Michael: I'll say again, just practising on demo accounts is really helpful. We care across some annoying roadblocks when actually trading. But this is good for you as we're trying to solve these problems so when you get there you know what to do.

Week Sixteen: 14ᵗʰ – 20ᵗʰ August 2017

LESSONS and LEARNINGS

Tier Two: Dog Investing

Taking action: PLACE those trades!

Michael's Choice

We waited for Gill to get her money invested – and to discover any pitfalls before we started on investing Michael's money!

One thing we realised pretty quickly was the amount of money lost on the exchange when buying the US stocks and whilst that was an appropriate cost with Gill's larger pot of money (nearly £200k) it felt like a huge amount from Michael's smaller amount.

As Gill's account was in sterling, we had to 'buy' the dollars to invest in the US 'Dogs of the Dow' – and that cost £3,887.50. Overall in Gill's portfolio that equated to 1.96% which is high.

Overall and over very long periods of time the two strategies – the 'Dogs of the FTSE' and of the Dow perform in very similar ways but the cost of buying the 'other', non-home currency could substantially eat into the profits – particularly if we had a smaller pot to play with. We should actually be able to make good this exchange cost over the next year or so but if we were investing with a smaller pot of money that would feel like a huge chunk of cost.

Therefore, only invest in different currencies after calculating the cost of the exchange! It is worth calling the broker about this as there are several ways to do this – you either buy the dollars (with sterling) as one lump and then invest from there – or you can buy dollars at each transaction or even buy overseas stocks in your home currency – just check the best way with your own broker.

Michael decided then to only do the 'Dogs of the FTSE' for now.

As before we took his pot of money – £35,000 and divided that over the 10 UK FTSE stocks and 'asked' the computer to buy £3,500 worth of shares – to include transaction and any trading costs.

Michael's Portfolio

We started with a clean £35k for Michael:

www.financialinvestingandtrading.com

We then invested it in the 10 UK 'Dogs' stocks between the 15ᵗʰ and 18ᵗʰ of August, investing as close to £3,500 per stock as we could. Again, we set the default investment to automatic reinvestment of any dividends.

Settlement Date	Date ↕	Description ◀	Reference	Debit	Credit
18/08/2017	16/08/2017	791 BP Del 4.46 S Date 18/08/17	KF45ZW		£3,558.39
17/08/2017	15/08/2017	1170 BT GRP Del 2.96 S Date 17/08/17	KF2ZZB		£3,497.34
17/08/2017	15/08/2017	1559 VODE GROU Del 2.23 S Date 17/08/17	KF2ZXZ		£3,499.65
17/08/2017	15/08/2017	78 ASTRAZENECA Del 44.46 S Date 17/08/17	KF2Z4Y		£3,491.56
17/08/2017	15/08/2017	109 IMPL BRAN Del 31.73 S Date 17/08/17	KF2Z4J		£3,482.55
17/08/2017	15/08/2017	159 ROYAL DUTB' Del 21.84 S Date 17/08/17	KF2Z4B		£3,496.22
17/08/2017	15/08/2017	231 GLAXOSMITHKLINE Del 14.99 S Date 17/08/17	KF2ZZW		£3,486.68
17/08/2017	15/08/2017	359 NATL GRID Del 9.66 S Date 17/08/17	KF2ZZM		£3,492.93
17/08/2017	15/08/2017	466 HSBC HDS Del 7.45 S Date 17/08/17	KF2Z2H		£3,497.21
17/08/2017	15/08/2017	162 ROYAL DUTCH'A' Del 21.41 S Date 17/08/17	KF2Z24		£3,493.25

113

Residual cash!

We tried very hard to invest every single penny of the cash here as any money left behind doesn't earn anything and isn't compounding up as we need it to in order to achieve either the annual target – or the long-term 'pension fund' target.

However, it is impossible to get 100% of the cash invested as the price of the share may differ (by very small fractions) in the time between you first press the 'order' button to when the order is actually filled.

In addition, dividends may be received on stocks which don't have the DRIP share option and those dividends come into the account as cash so it is very likely you will build up a small cash deposit over time.

Unless this cash deposit is large enough to take a separate transaction together with a transaction cost then it's best to leave these small amounts alone and just add them into your next selection when you review the 'Dogs' after one year. In that case, just take the amount you have available for the new selection, add in the available cash balance, and invest that in total into the new share.

No doubt that will STILL leave you with a few pence or cents left behind but that's all.

If, when you do your 'Dogs' selection criteria at the end of the year, there are no shares to be exchanged then if the residual cash amount is small just leave it again for the following year – but if it's large enough to take a transaction and its cost then just buy as many shares as you can of the CHEAPEST share on your list of 10.

114

Michael's Portfolio

Michael managed to get his £35,000 almost entirely invested and he only had £4.22 left over at the end of his buying spree! This is the transaction record:

Settlement Date	Date	Description	Reference	Debit	Credit	Running Balance
18/08/2017	16/08/2017	791 BP PAR Del 4.46 S Date 18/08/17	KF452W	£3,558.39		£4.22
17/08/2017	15/08/2017	1170 BT GROUP PAR Del 2.96 S Date 17/08/17	KF222B	£3,497.34		£3,562.61
17/08/2017	15/08/2017	1559 VODE GROU Del 2.23 S Date 17/08/17	KF22X2	£3,499.65		£7,059.95
17/08/2017	15/08/2017	78 ASTRA ZENE PAR Del 44.46 S Date 17/08/17	KF22AV	£3,491.56		£10,559.60
17/08/2017	15/08/2017	109 IMPL BRAN PAR Del 31.73 S Date 17/08/17	KF2241	£3,482.55		£14,051.16
17/08/2017	15/08/2017	159 ROYAL DUT B Del 21.84 S Date 17/08/17	KF224E	£3,496.22		£17,533.71
17/08/2017	15/08/2017	231 GLAXOSMIT PAR Del 14.99 S Date 17/08/17	KF22ZW	£3,486.69		£21,029.93
17/08/2017	15/08/2017	359 NAT. GRID PAR Del 9.66 S Date 17/08/17	KF222M	£3,492.93		£24,516.61
17/08/2017	15/08/2017	466 HSBC HLDG PAR Del 7.45 S Date 17/08/17	KF222H	£3,497.21		£28,009.54
17/08/2017	15/08/2017	162 ROYAL DUTCH 'A' Del 21.41 S Date 17/08/17	KF2224	£3,493.25		£31,506.75

Summary: Tier Two

We now have a strategy in place that should serve us for a lifetime! We have put our lump sums of money into Tier Two and have our small regular savings going into the Tier One strategy.

With those two strategies we should be able to generate our 10% target without any further input from us but we don't want the experiment to stop here.

We are keen to see quite how much more than the 10% we could generate with a bit more knowledge, so we're now having a short holiday and break before heading into Tier Three – which is still a capital investing strategy but it needs more time and knowledge to implement.

We've also got a broker account open which we will be able to use for the next stage of investing, so we're all set to go!

Daily Diary

Michael: When I first learnt about this strategy and researched its past returns, I knew I would put my pension fund into it. I was impressed and enjoyed the maths side of it. It is really simple and the returns speak for themselves. It is just a shame that so few people know about it and it's a shame that investing in this way is seen as inaccessible. Since finding out about it I've been recommending it to family and friends and I'm glad we've got this far. I would say that the key is sticking with it. When you immerse yourself it's much easier. I really think this is something anyone could do and should do with their savings.

Gill: I'm very proud of my "boy" and it makes me realise that we could easily educate every young person to make simple, but effective, investments.

I'm now on holiday for five weeks - time to relax!

4. Tier Three

Week Twenty-Two: 25ᵗʰ September – 1ˢᵗ October 2017

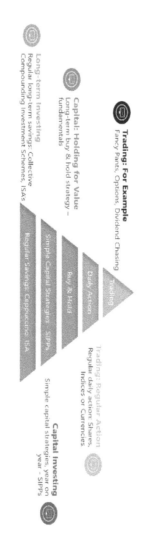

Tier Three is the middle Tier of our Pyramid and is the Tier where we need to start studying a little more, and we certainly need to know more than the very basic level that we need for Tiers One and Two.

In order to justify that learning we need to ensure then, that we can achieve a greater return on our money than the 10% per annum we are pretty certain about with Tiers One and Two. The first two tiers are almost completely passive: apart from a little activity at the very beginning. Then with annual tweaks, these strategies more or less run themselves and can be left for the very long term – and retirement if that's your aim.

Tier Three requires more input, is more active and requires regular review, but a rough guide is that the input needs to be quite regular when looking for shares to buy, and then perhaps monthly thereafter. Tier Three is still a long term 'hold' strategy and doesn't need constant or regular buying and selling of shares. If we pick the right shares for the right reasons, they should be pretty secure for the short and medium term to be left alone to grow.

The most famous 'buy and hold' expert is of course Warren Buffet, who claims that his favourite holding period is 'for ever'! Now that causes a little issue for us normal folk – because eventually we need the money back, so the forever holding period isn't really practical but we need to assume that were going to hold these shares for at least a few years.

"Someone is sitting in the shade today because someone planted a tree a long time ago."
- Warren Buffett

The Buffet approach though is obviously sound – after all it made him the richest man on Earth for many years – and what he looks for are the solid basics of a company or business that he believes will ensure steady and consistent growth over time. Those basics are called the **fundamentals.**

Every expert investor has their key areas of a business to review and monitor where they aim to identify the key factors that will create success. There are 8 key areas to look at to start with, some financial and some not and we will look at them all in this and the next session.

Where to find the fundamentals

The internet is obviously our first resource and as well as just inputting criteria into a search engine and following the links we can also go back to our broker account which we opened for the Tier Two 'Dogs' investments, to get some basic data.

TD Ameritrade has a research page where we can start, and if we click on 'stock profile' that will provide us with the fundamental information.

Also on the Interactive Investor broker site we can input any stock to get relevant information.

Once you click on the share or stock you are interested in looking at, data will then appear.

I've downloaded the basic research page below that appeared when I entered just *'Coc'* – I'm searching for details about Coca-Cola here – it gives me a drop down menu of all the potential Coca-Cola shares to look at.

I've highlighted the UK version of the stock, near the bottom – it says LSE (London Stock Exchange) in the title description. The first company that comes up on the search is the American version of the share – and there it says NYSE (New York Stock Exchange) in the title description.

portfolio ▾   trading ▾   cash & transfers ▾   research ▾

FTSE 100 7697.77 0   FTSE 250 20726.26 0   FTSE TechMark 4681.3 0   Dow Jones 24719.

research > UK company research

Quick Search

coc

Coca-Cola Enterprises, Inc - NYSE:CCE

Coca-Cola Amatil Ltd - ASX:CCL

Coca-Cola Bottling Co Consolidated - NASDAQ:COKE

Coca-Cola Co - NYSE:KO

Coca-Cola Co - XETR:CCC3

Coca-Cola European Partners PLC - XAMS:CCE

Coca-Cola European Partners PLC - XMCE:CCE

Coca-Cola European Partners PLC - NYSE:CCE

Coca-Cola Femsa SAB de CV ADR - NYSE:KOF

Coca-Cola HBC AG - LSE:CCH

Cochlear Ltd - ASX:COM

Stock Selector

We bring you a range of advanced stock selection tools that scan the Morningstar stock database:

Growth Stocks
Income Stocks
Momentum Stocks
Value Stocks

Calculators

Share Price
Share Price Lookup
Historic Share Price
Accumulated Share Price

the information provided by Morningstar is correct but it neither warrants, represents nor guarantees the contents o
e   ns or any inconsistencies herein.

© Copyright 2018 Morningstar. All rights reserved.

And when I click on the share I want to research I get a header or summary page, plus links to countless pages of data!

Unless we wanted to research this data on a full-time basis we need to home in on a few key areas and they are our 'fundamentals' to investigate.

Coca-Cola HBC AG CCH

Buy Sell

Stock Report PDF

Overview | Chart | Prices | Performance | Key Dates | Ratios | Contact Details | Financials | Advisors | Brokers | News | Owners | Analysis | Insiders

Overview

Summary | Prices | Performance | Key Dates | Ratios | Contact Details | Financials | Advisors | Brokers | News | Owners | Analysis | Insiders

Last Price
GBX **2,420.00** ↑ **6.00|0.25%**
Day Change

As of 29/12/2017
12:35:05 GMT GBX
Minimum 15 Minutes Delay.

Last Close Price	2,414.00p
ISIN	CH0198251305

| Day Range | 2,397.00 - 2,439.00 |
| Volume | 208,949 |

| Mkt Cap | 8.81Bil |
| P/E | Infinity |

| 52-Wk Range | 1,729.00 - 2,682.00 |
| P/S | 1.72 |

| Yield % | 1.41 |
| P/CF | 15.33 |

Share Price

■ Price Chart (GBX)
■ Coca-Cola HBC AG

2017 | Aug | Sep | Oct | Nov | Dec
1D 5D 1M 3M 6M YTD 1Y 3Y 5Y Max

2,700
2,600
2,500
2,400
2,300
2,200
2,100

Company Profile

Coca-Cola HBC AG through its subsidiary is engaged in the production, selling and distribution of non-alcoholic ready-to-drink beverages under the franchise from the Coca-Cola Company.

Sector	Consumer Defensive
Industry	Beverages - Soft Drinks
Market Position	54 of 1836 Companies
Index	FTSE 100, FTSE 350, FTSE All Share

N.B. When researching, always make sure to look at independent reviews and websites as the generated information on a company's own website is likely to be positively presented (and possibly distorted).

The fundamentals

There are EIGHT areas to look at, and the first one is:

1) **Size**: the size of a company is measured by its market capitalisation – the Market Cap we discussed in an earlier session. As a reminder this is calculated by multiplying the number of shares in issue by the current share price. Therefore, if a share price drops so does the company's Market Cap.

   We are only considering investing in larger public companies here and the smallest market cap company that we are likely to be reviewing is a minimum of £100m or $250m – and this would be VERY small for a public company.

   At the other end of the scale the market cap of Coca-Cola Enterprises is $191 billion and HSBC (the largest Market Cap company on the London Stock Exchange) is £152 billion.

   To get onto any list of larger quoted companies the Market Cap of a company would need to be about £/$ 1 billion.

   So what?

   What we are partly looking for is reassurance that the company is large enough to sustain itself and has – by definition – a track record of some growth. And were also looking for some evidence that it can continue to grow further – so to see it has potential scope for expansion.

   Therefore, as long as the company being reviewed has a Market Cap of somewhere between £/$ 1 billion and say, £/$ 50 billion, we know that it has reached a critical mass in terms of size, but has room to grow further.

As we get more knowledgeable we could develop this into a strategy all of its own and select shares within a certain size band with expectations of growth, but for now all we need is reassurance that the company is big enough and therefore unlikely to get onto difficulty in the very near future. And then we can investigate further.

Daily Diary

Gill: I'm a mathematician at heart and any part of a strategy that I can create that has numbers in it has a certain logic to it and makes me happy! I can see that I could create a spreadsheet of the eight fundamentals and measure them and create a scoring or ranking system of potential investments – woohoo!

Michael: I think this strategy comes with time as your knowledge of the markets grows. For example, you start to know which companies are on the way up (say, tech companies). You will also start to know particular stocks very well; they could be something you are interested in or work with. This comes with time, so don't worry if it feels alien at the beginning.

Week Twenty-Three: 2nd – 8th October 2017

LESSONS and LEARNINGS

Tier Three: The Fundamentals

After size, we want to look at the financial fundamentals:

1) **Profitability:** For our level of investing the company has to be profitable! In the future we could look at loss making companies as they could offer a much greater return as they move into profitability but for now that is too high a risk.

   Ideally we also want to see profitability rising a little which could indicate operational efficiencies. I have downloaded here the research page profitability of ratios of Cisco Systems:

Cisco Systems Inc CSCO

Buy | Sell

Margins (% of Sales)

	2013	2014	2015	2016	2017
Revenue	100.00%	100.00%	100.00%	100.00%	100.00%
Cost of Revenue	39.43%	41.09%	39.62%	37.13%	37.04%
Gross Margin	**60.57%**	**58.91%**	**60.38%**	**62.87%**	**62.96%**
SG&A	24.28%	24.26%	24.13%	23.22%	23.28%
Research and development	12.22%	13.35%	12.63%	12.78%	12.62%
Operating Margin	**23.03%**	**19.82%**	**21.91%**	**25.71%**	**24.94%**
Net Int, Inc and Other	46.13%	40.43%	44.69%	51.94%	50.54%
EBT Margin	**23.10%**	**20.61%**	**22.78%**	**26.24%**	**25.60%**

Profitability

	2013	2014	2015	2016	2017
Tax Rate	2.56%	3.95%	4.52%	4.43%	5.58%
Net Margin	20.54%	16.66%	18.27%	21.81%	20.02%
Return on Assets	**10.35**	**7.61**	**8.22**	**9.13**	**7.64**
Financial Leverage	1.71	1.86	1.90	1.91	1.96
Return on Equity	**18.08**	**13.57**	**15.44**	**17.42**	**14.81**

We need to review at least 5 years' data so that we can identify trends and comparisons within the company itself, and when looking at profitability it doesn't really matter which line you look at as long as you look at the same line over all the years to ascertain a growth or consistency in the figures.

The main profitability figures are:

Gross Margin	Sales less direct costs of sale
Net Margin	Sales less direct costs less overheads
EBT	Earnings before Tax
EBITDA	Earnings before Interest payments, Tax, Depreciation and Amortization

Just choose one you like the sound of and compare across the board!

If we highlight the NET margin figures from CISCO for instance we can see that over the years the figures have been:

	2013	2104	2015	2016	2107
Net Margin	20.54%	16.66%	18.27%	21.81%	20.02%

And from that we can see a dip in 2014 which has been recovering since then. All years are profitable and even 16.66% margin seems relatively high so CISCO looks OK for profitability.

You need to set a bench mark of profitability as a minimum benchmark. For me, I always want to see at least 10% margin of profitability, partly because I know that's an approximate standard for margin across all business types and also because 10% is my own personal target for returns – and if I can do it then

I expect these companies to do it too.

Sometimes there is an explanation of why profitability has dropped, so we need to read the reports as well to pick up any reasons for fluctuations and also to pick up the company 'mood and confidence'.

Ideally, we want to see words such as, 'positive', 'exciting', 'growing', 'exceeding expectations', 'favourable' and so on. It's fairly easy to put a word search check on a company report to pick up these words – and also the opposite or negative ones.

Set a target to find say, 10 positive statements in the accounts before a company gets added to your possible investment list, and adjust that number and list as you get more experienced.

In short, what we are looking for in profitability is a stable or growing trend and the right words!

2) **Dividends**: we know that dividends are the income paid out of profits from a business and if those dividends are regular, or increasing a little, it gives us an indication that the company is thriving and worth our investment.

   Dividends are paid for each individual share and if we look at Cisco dividend history (available on one of those links from the research page at the brokers website) we can see all the information we need:

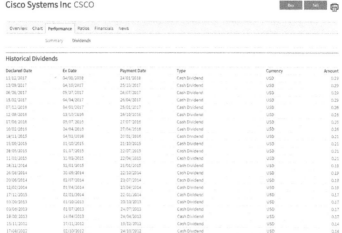

Historical Dividends

Declared Date	Ex Date	Payment Date	Type	Currency	Amount
11/12/2017	04/01/2018	24/01/2018	Cash Dividend	USD	0.29
13/09/2017	04/10/2017	25/10/2017	Cash Dividend	USD	0.29
06/06/2017	05/07/2017	26/07/2017	Cash Dividend	USD	0.29
15/02/2017	04/04/2017	26/04/2017	Cash Dividend	USD	0.29
07/12/2016	04/01/2017	25/01/2017	Cash Dividend	USD	0.26
12/09/2016	03/10/2016	26/10/2016	Cash Dividend	USD	0.26
07/06/2016	05/07/2016	27/07/2016	Cash Dividend	USD	0.26
10/02/2016	04/04/2016	27/04/2016	Cash Dividend	USD	0.26
18/11/2015	04/01/2016	20/01/2016	Cash Dividend	USD	0.21
15/09/2015	01/10/2015	21/10/2015	Cash Dividend	USD	0.21
20/05/2015	01/07/2015	22/07/2015	Cash Dividend	USD	0.21
11/02/2015	31/03/2015	22/04/2015	Cash Dividend	USD	0.21
18/11/2014	02/01/2015	21/01/2015	Cash Dividend	USD	0.19
26/08/2014	30/09/2014	22/10/2014	Cash Dividend	USD	0.19
20/06/2014	02/07/2014	23/07/2014	Cash Dividend	USD	0.19
12/02/2014	01/04/2014	23/04/2014	Cash Dividend	USD	0.19
17/12/2013	02/01/2014	22/01/2014	Cash Dividend	USD	0.17
03/09/2013	01/10/2013	23/10/2013	Cash Dividend	USD	0.17
03/06/2013	01/07/2013	24/07/2013	Cash Dividend	USD	0.17
28/03/2013	04/04/2013	24/04/2013	Cash Dividend	USD	0.17
15/11/2012	27/11/2012	19/12/2012	Cash Dividend	USD	0.14
17/08/2012	02/10/2012	24/10/2012	Cash Dividend	USD	0.14

The dividend has risen from 0.14 cents per share in 2012 to 0.29 cents per share in 2017, and we can also see that a dividend has been paid quarterly, which is unusual.

This type of dividend record demonstrates stability and strength in a company, and if there's no dividend at all – find out why!

3) **The P/E ratio**: the P/E ratio is the price earnings ratio and is intended to give us an idea of how long we would need to wait to get our investment back. It is broadly a calculation of what we earn from the investment compared to the price.

The Price Earnings Ratio is:

The Share price divided by the EPS (Earning per Share)

Where

EPS = earnings ÷ total shares outstanding

Example: If a company has net earnings of say, £1m and 1,000,000 shares in issue then its EPS is: £1,000,000/1,000,000 = 1

Then if the share price was £10, then its P/E ratio would be:

£10/1 = 10

What that means is that it would take 10 years of earnings as they are to recover the price of a share £1 EPS: share price is £10 = 10 years to equalise.

You can calculate it from scratch yourself or just look it up as the P/E ratio is always one of the first pieces of information any website will give you about a share.

If we go back to our research on Cisco we can see that the P/E ratio is firmly on the front page of the research and is quoted at 19.95.

P/E ratio pointers:

* The bigger the number the higher the company is valued.

* Lower numbers suggest room for growth.

* As at the end of 2016, the P/E ratio of the combined FTSE 100 was 33 (compared to an historical average of 15).

Cisco Systems Inc CSCO

Buy Sell

| Overview | Chart | Performance | Ratios | Financials | News |

Summary

Last Price
$38.30 ↓ -0.29 | -0.75%

As of 29/12/2017
19:47:01 EST | USD
Minimum 15 Minutes Delay.

Day Change		

Last Close Price	**Day Range**	**Mkt Cap**	**52-Wk Range**	**Yield %**
38.59	38.30 - 38.62	189.30Bil	29.80 - 39.00	2.95

ISIN	**Volume**	**P/E**	**P/S**	**P/CF**
US17275R1023	12,583,621	19.95	4.03	13.54

⇨

www.financialinvestingandtrading.com

P/E Ratio:
Buts:

* It can be calculated in many different ways using historical earnings or projected future (estimated) earnings, therefore

* It's only really useful to compare to itself or other companies in the same sector.

4) **Debt**: a certain amount of debt is clearly appropriate in businesses as they use the borrowings to expand, but the levels of debt have to be appropriate. Suggestions are that its debt shouldn't be bigger than 3–5 years' annual earnings – so that means a company can pay off its debt in 3–5 years.

   Calculating debt is very difficult as it can be described in many ways and the figures can be difficult to find in company reports and so I suggest that you just read the commentary section on any research pages to see if the level of debt is mentioned. If the level of debt is a problem then the commentators will pick that up and say so!

Summary

Those four financial areas of profitability, dividends, P/E and debt, will give you a general sense of how strong a company is, and they will all feature highly in any business review of any company. You should certainly consider these areas before you invest. However, a business is about a lot more than its numbers, and we will address those areas in the next session.

Daily Diary

Gill: I used to think that I needed to calculate all these numbers myself – so I'm mightily relieved to know that I can just look them all up in the click of a link!

Michael: This shows how many factors go into price changes and why Tier Three is one of the hardest Tiers. But once the research is done and you've bought a share, it becomes quite passive again.

Week Twenty-Four: 9th - 15th October 2017

LESSONS and LEARNINGS

Tier Three: The Fundamentals

There are two areas to investigate before we buy any share in any company – the financial side of the business and then there's the customer side. What any business needs to do is to keep getting orders and sales and for that they need customers and there are four areas to look at here:

1) **Likeability:** ask yourself; do you actually **like** what the business does, and do you – or would you – spend your hard-earned cash to buy their product or services? There have been many famous examples of people liking the product so much 'they bought the company', probably the most well known is the Victor Kiam adverts in the late 1970s for Remington Razors, but there have been others and in fact, if Warren Buffet 'likes' a product he just buys more and more of their shares. I'm not suggesting we go and buy whole companies here but do you like their product enough to buy a share or two? It's a good indicator if you do.

2) **Understanding:** do you understand what the company does? If you don't, then don't buy their

shares because you won't understand what they're saying in reports and on their website, and that can be dangerous if there's negative news particularly.

This principle holds true for investing only and once you get past that and onto trading (upper Tiers of the Pyramid) then it doesn't matter what they do but for now, stick to shares of companies who sell a product that you can broadly understand.

3) **Access:** deliberately go and experience how a customer gets access to the product or service. Go into the retail shop, stay at the hotel or eat at the restaurant and see how you feel about the ease of access to the product or service. Many shops just overload their outlets with stock – so much so that you can't actually get a dress off the rack or a book off the shelf to look at it. That's disastrous as many customers will just leave the shop from frustration and never buy.

Perhaps more importantly nowadays is to visit their online shop and browse around their website. What you are looking for is ease of use and simple progress to the shopping basket and purchasing buttons.

If you find the website easy to navigate and buy from, then so will others.

Keep looking at the access point – physical shops and online – is the stock regularly updated? Is the website fresh and new? It all helps to encourage sales and orders and higher profits.

If you can't test their access points and ease of sales, let's say it's a major industrial chemical company where you have no interaction and where there is no 'online shop', read other market reviews to see if anything is mentioned here and then try and find some customer feedback.

4) **Customer review and feedback:** in our social media world, poor customer service is flashed around the globe in the blink of an eye and so if a company is poor at their customer care then you should easily be able to find that. But be careful because negative voices tend to shout longer and louder than positive ones. Also, social media reviews can be faked and distorted.

In any case, a poor review isn't necessarily the end of the selection process, and we should also look at how the company deals with the complaint or difficulty. It's often said that a complainant dealt with properly becomes a customer for life because the company has proved that they listen and take appropriate action.

Customer reviews come in several forms, and the best feedback you can get is:

a) Direct from an existing customer that has been either face to face or on the phone. Try to go and look at a product or service provided.

b) Existing customer testimonials – often in video form nowadays on websites – and make sure there is some identification given of the customer – not necessarily the full name and address but an identification that you could use if you decided to phone the company and say 'Who was that? Can I speak to them?'

c) Independent reviews from say, market research companies or journalists, as these people will be able to give you the background of their report.

d) Trader review websites as again, sometimes you can actually see photos of 'products' or 'services' delivered.

e) Personal reviews on major websites reviewing say, holidays or restaurants are acceptable at some level, but they can be faked or distorted so shouldn't be your only form of check.

Customer feedback is so vital to any business that you can't leave a restaurant nowadays without the server urging you to post a comment about them or the restaurant 'online'.

Summary

This non-financial review of a potential investment is just as important as the financial review. The facts and figures talk about the past and account for what has happened and this customer based review looks at the future and the business potential.

What we want to see is a pattern of sustainability of customers who can buy easily and regularly, and that keeps up the sales and the money to keep the company going and growing.

Finally, what the customer wants to see is consistency – they want to know that every time they access the product or service it's going to be the same, or as good as it was before. When they are reassured of that they repeat buy constantly because the certainty makes them feel relaxed and they buy more easily.

One simple example of this is shop opening hours.

When a business is small the shop owner will often have irregular opening hours because that can keep costs down but sadly, if a customer goes to your door and finds the shop shut they are less likely to come back because they now feel uncertain and unsettled about the access point.

And finally, a note about consistency – the most consistent products worldwide are products such as McDonald's or Coca-Cola. We know that wherever in the world we are – even if we're in very unfamiliar territory – as soon as we see a sign for one of those products we know EXACTLY what we're going to be able to get and buy.

All we need to do now is to create a checklist of our 4 financial criteria and our 4 customer criteria and set a target to achieve say 5 or 6 or all 8 positive criteria before we will consider investing in the shares.

Daily Diary

Gill: I believe people hugely underestimate this customer side of business evaluation. I've always believed that if I don't like a product or service then there's a chance others won't either – and that impacts financial success.

Michael: It's easier to understand stocks you have an interest in so choose an industry you either work in or know a lot about to start with. All these non-financial criteria show how important public sentiment can be. So another way to gauge public view is just from the news.

Week Twenty-Five: 16th – 22nd October 2017

LESSONS and LEARNINGS

Tier Three: The Fundamentals

We now have a checklist of 8 fundamental items to check for a company – after we've checked their size, of course – to help us decide if we want to invest or not.

1) Profitability

2) Dividends

3) The P/E Ratio

4) Debt

5) Likeability

6) Understanding

7) Access

8) Customer review and feedback

And now we need some way of narrowing down the number of companies we look at – after all, this is still meant to be fairly passive as an activity.

Fortunately, there are hundreds of people constantly researching all the fundamentals of all the main companies all the time – and they get paid for doing so!

They constantly and regularly publish their thoughts and findings in a variety of newsletters, tips services and portfolios and so for us, at this stage of our learning, I suggest we just look at those recommendations and pick one or two shares to watch and then check them against our list of 8 criteria and 'dummy' invest and see what happens.

Our small amount of knowledge, combined with the expertise of the industry experts, should mean that we can make a few decent investments over time and I tried this technique with a class of 50 people recently and every single one of their shares resulted in a profit at some point since.

Where to get tips?

1) **On the web**: there are many share tipping websites and I've just put share tips into a search engine on my computer and there are 399 million results!

2) **The brokers**: We need to reduce that massive list before we can start to do any research of our own, and one place we can look is the broker that we have our account with and they all publish regular newsletters and share tips.

For instance, on the TD Ameritrade website there is an ideas link in their research area with recommendations. In the UK, brokers e-mail out recommendation newsletters on a weekly basis.

Two that I personally look at are:

http://www.hl.co.uk/shares/share-research/share-tips

This is a service from Hargreaves Lansdown and I like this one as it refers to other sources and journals and therefore has a collective judgement.

And of course interactive investor.
http://www.iii.co.uk/articles/469655/six-share-tips-2018

where they include a guide as to the risk and speculative exposure to each share as well.

Here is an example of a share tips newsletter.

Six share tips for 2018

*By **Lee Wild** | Sun, 24th December 2017 - 10:00*

Investors would typically be happy with share prices at a record high and positive returns from domestic stockmarkets. However, the UK's single-digit gains in 2017 were dwarfed by stellar returns in the US and the performance of alternative assets such as bitcoin, up over 1,000%.

Brexit remains a cap on investment and economic growth, and sterling is up 9% versus the dollar, but there's not much wrong with UK equities. Yes, they're not cheap, but profits are growing and talk of overvaluation is a distraction.

So how did our 2017 speculative tips fare?

Software systems firm **Scisys** (SSY) was our top-performing growth tip of 2017, having returned 42% by mid-November.

Markets liked the firm's strong results, big contract wins and €18 million (£13 million) of work on the German national satellite communications mission in October.

Within a month of tipping **Mysale** (MYSL), the online shopping club's share price had risen by 38% following a knockout first-half update. That was a highlight, but there's still lots to like about the business.

Global trends in technology were meant to drive growth at **Software Quality Services** (SQS), but results in March told a different story, amid a shift to shorter-term digital projects. The shares fell 18%, but, just as results began to improve, the company accepted an all-cash bid from German firm Assystem Technologies, valuing SQS at 825p. That's 36% higher than our tip price this time last year!

Our trio of speculative income stocks did what we picked them to do. **Legal & General** (LGEN) yielded 6.1% and returned a 12% capital gain. **Galliford Try** (GFRD) and **Greene King** (GNK) yielded 7.4% and 5% respectively, but their share prices fell.

Speculative Growth

In every case, please do **NOT** rely just on the tip itself – use their information as a starting point to check against your own criteria.

3) **Tips services**: as well as tips from the web or from brokers, there are specialist tips services and you would normally pay for these. It may be a subscription to a share tips magazine or to a members only website, and share tips services effectively 'sell' you the hottest tip.

4) **Newspapers and journals** will however give you their tips for the price of the journal or newspaper and all quality newspapers have at least an annual tipping service, which is generally also accompanied by a report on last year's tips, which can be enlightening and is certainly some evidence for us to check before we take their view on board.

For instance, this is the annual review from The Times newspaper on how they did in 2017:

Tempus tips 2017: how they fared

Company	Sector	Share price Dec 30, 2016	Yesterday	Change
Premier Oil	Natural resources	74p	76¼p	+4.1%
Bunzl	Support services	£21.09	£20.58	-2.5%
Nex Group	Banking and finance	464½p	601p	+29.7%
Burford Capital	Banking and finance	572½p	£11.65	+102.6%
Sirius Minerals	Natural resources	19¼p	23p	+19.5%
Capita	Support services	531p	405¾p	-23.7%
Meggitt	Engineering	458½p	483p	+5.5%
Merlin Entertainments	Leisure	448½p	360¼p	-19.6%
Thomas Cook	Leisure	87¼p	121p	+39%
RPC Group	Support services	994p	870p	-12%

FTSE All share index gain **8.1%**   Average portfolio gain **14.3%**

Source: Thomson Reuters *Percentage change based on the closing price on Dec 28

But, as before, still check the facts and figures used as it is very easy to report slightly different prices (mid, offer, bid etc) which would make a difference to the stated return or growth.

N.B. *Qualified tips that come from experienced reporters or journalist who put their views in a public domain like this should ALWAYS be above average – otherwise they shouldn't be doing their job – and this 14.3% return, although it looks high when compared to the FTSE All Share, would be 'normal' for these types of reports and I have seen 2017 annual reports showing 40% - 50% price increases over the year.*

5) **Portfolios**: many of the tips services, brokers, papers and journals also offer a portfolio tips service and this is where they select a whole group of shares to invest in. Some of them are quite sophisticated and they do normally have a risk ranking – so a portfolio might be for small tech stocks with high growth potential but little track record, for instance. Some portfolios are for growth and income, some are geographically based, some are sector based and so on.

As before, there is some merit in following a portfolio selection but as before, there are pitfalls. The selector may just be having a bad year – even if their track record for the past decade is good. Also, in many cases you have to keep following the portfolio tips selections as the "expert" will buy and sell from the portfolio on a regular basis and unless you keep up and keep doing the same buys and sells then your version of the portfolio will get out of line.

As part of the research for this learning Michael monitored a portfolio created 5 years ago where he clearly did NOT make the regular changes and after 5 years the portfolio was broadly bust!

Tier Three summary

At this third Tier of investing it should be fairly easy to beat the 10% return generated passively from Tiers One and Two but it does take a little more effort.

The simplest way to get started at this Tier is to follow some selections from tried and tested experts, who should all be beating the standard market return fairly comprehensively – and in the main they do.

However, this is not to be a slavish following without thought or review.

Start with the selections or tips by all means but then add your own review: take the 8 selection criteria we have created – 4 financial and 4 customer based – and add your own additional layer of scrutiny to make the selections you personally are happy with and believe in.

Invest small at first until you get more experience and watch the shares fairly regularly – either weekly or monthly – to make sure that everything is going to plan. Set yourself a win loss target – so there's no point in just selling the share if it falls a little in value – they all do that from time to time – but work out how much you're prepared to lose and what profit target you want.

An illustration of this might be to risk, or be prepared to lose, 5% on the losers but aim to gain 10% on the winners for instance – you decide.

And we will pick up these learnings in the next section where we go onto TRADING.

So far, we have only covered the first Three Tiers of investing where our objective is to make slow and steady capital growth over long periods of time by accessing the major share markets through an index or by sifting out some individual shares from the group. Trading however is completely different and can be used to generate regular income from regular time input.

We will cover that in Tiers Four and Five.

Daily Diary

Gill: I firmly believe that with some knowledge any 'normal' person can outperform any tipster but letting them do all the hard work and research first certainly works for me!

Michael: Now we know what we are looking at you'll start to see stock recommendations everywhere. However, now we know how to choose which ones are the best investments.

5. Tier Four - Part One

Week Twenty-Six: 23rd – 29th October 2017

LESSONS and LEARNINGS

Tier FOUR

So far we have only covered the generation of capital – at a target rate of 10% per annum – where money is passively invested in shares for long periods of time, either regularly or as one lump sum.

At Tier Four we can start to look at generating regular income from regular activity and review, but we need to increase our knowledge if we want increased returns on our money.

In the first Three Tiers we were interested in what the share was but at Tier Four, we don't care! Broadly, with **investing,** we need to know what the share is but with **trading** it doesn't matter and we're more interested in <u>how</u> it moves and why. Frankly, we could trade anything – shares, currency, commodities and so on, because all we need to know is **how** the price is moving and take advantage of that.

There are the three things that can impact a price when trading, and they are:

- Fundamentals
- Sentiment and
- Technicals.

Fundamentals

Now the term fundamentals has a variety of meanings and having just learned one meaning – in connection with the fundamentals of a share in respect to the general financial health and strength of a company: dividends, profit, sales growth, level of corporate debt, customer feedback and so on, we now need to learn a second meaning.

I've now discovered that the term fundamentals applies to many different things and at different levels!

The original concept of 'fundamentals' affecting a company and individual share trading are still right but there are also national fundamentals and even global fundamentals that affect trading and price movements.

National Fundamentals

National fundamentals are, broadly, interest rates, GDP and inflation! And these three things are completely interlinked and the management of them is a fine balancing act performed by the Government and the Bank of England in the UK, or the Federal Reserve in the US, or the Regulating Bank or Body for each country.

That balancing act is controlled via the base interest rate, which rose back up to 0.5% in the UK in 2017, and back up to 1.5% in the US.

The base interest rate is used as the balancing factor because:

When base rates are low:

a)   People borrow more because borrowing is cheap, and

b)   They spend more – so GDP (Gross Domestic product – the measure of an economie's growth) goes up as the economy expands because people are spending more, and

c)   As spending and demand increases we create inflation.

As a result of increased inflation, interest rates are raised, and

When base rates are high:

a)   People borrow less because they're fearful and they can't afford it and

b)   They also spend less, the economy starts to stagnate or even contract (which is a recession) and

c)   Demand falls which results in prices being reduced and Inflation goes down.

AND as base rates rise, currency tends to get stronger and this makes a country's exports more expensive and less attractive to overseas buyers and that also slows the economy.

And as a result of reduced growth interest rates are lowered, and… The cycle continues!

Interest rates, GDP and inflation!

Interest rates, GDP and inflation are a constant balancing act. If inflation is too high that is bad for the economy long term so the Regulator (Bank of England in the UK) raises interest rates so that inflation slows.

But if there is too little inflation, the economy slows

down and needs a boost which is given by lowering interest rates (so people borrow and spend) and the economy picks up.

It's a very fine line of action and reaction: if base rates are too high the economy falls; if base rates are too low then inflation rises.

In addition, our national economy doesn't always react to a base rate change in the same way because it depends on other factors: the confidence of the people and external, global influences. A base rate rise today will not necessarily create the same outcome as a base rate rise a decade ago.

In the UK, the main measure is inflation. The Bank of England try and keep inflation at 2% or just below. At that level they feel we are in balance as an economy. Any base interest rate movements are generally tied to achieving that aim of 2% inflation. The rate of inflation in the UK rose to approximately 3% in 2017 which was above the target of 2% and consequently, the Bank of England raised interest rates.

They will monitor the outcome or impact of that rise and if inflation starts to come down they will leave the base rate alone, but if inflation stays high then another base rate rise is likely.

Just remember, when interest rates go up, the economy needs medical attention!

So What!

I want to be a trader, not an economist! However, these national fundamentals provide an indication of what we expect trades to do: when the fundamentals are strong then we expect prices (of shares, indices and currencies) to rise and when the fundamentals are weak we expect prices to fall.

But these national fundamentals are just one piece of the jigsaw: the strongest trades are when the fundamentals AND the sentiment AND the technical signs all support each other.

The fundamentals are an indicator – but just one – we also want to find the other parts of our F + S + T formula before we trade.

Summary

We now know that there are fundamentals for:

- an individual company: profit, dividends etc
- a market sector – say pharmaceuticals (drug regulation for instance)

And these affect INVESTING more, and there are also fundamentals for:

- a country (interest rates, GDP and inflation)
- the world at large (for instance, US base rate changes will have some impact on other countries and markets)

And these last two fundamentals affect our TRADING more.

DAILY DIARY

Gill: I've always thought that understanding the larger economy was impossible but now I can see that if we follow those three basic things then we can understand all that we need to know.

Michael: This is the first difference between trading and investing. You've got to keep up to date with the news to know the fundamentals and make sure you keep an eye on your trades.

Week Twenty-Seven: 30th October – 5th November 2017

LESSONS and LEARNINGS

We now know that there are three things that can impact a trade, and they are:

- Fundamentals
- Sentiment and
- Technicals.

We have covered the Fundamentals before and now we can look at the Sentiment part of the equation.

Sentiment

Sentiment is purely a human activity which indicates if we are happy, positive and confident to invest or not. This positivity is partly gained from the amount of faith an investor has in the major global or national fundamentals.

When humans are buoyant and upbeat they invest in equities, commodities and currency. When they are fearful and downbeat they move their money out of those investments (which are perceived as 'risky') and put their money into fixed interest government or high grade corporate bonds or commodities like gold, where the return is 'guaranteed' but low.

The more confident people are, in their money or microeconomy, or in the larger national or macroeconomy, the greater the risk they will take with investments and they will buy equities and currency, where the return can be higher but unknown.

This is called being Risk ON.

Conversely, when people are fearful (say when North Korea do a nuclear test – or when they hear poor economic forecasts) they do the opposite: they sell equities and currency and put their money into fixed interest bonds which are perceived to be safer.

This is called being RISK OFF.

However, it's not as clear cut as this and a market doesn't go from being Risk ON to Risk OFF in a heartbeat, it's a more gradual movement from one end of a risk scale to another.

The sentiment in the market moves gradually as the humans gain – or lose - faith in the fundamentals.

The stronger the sentiment is, the more likely the

projected movements arising from the fundamentals will play out and create a trade that we can profit from.

Causes of sentiment

Sentiment is caused – as with the fundamentals – either globally or nationally, and arise, in the main, from political or economic activity.

The USA tends to drive global sentiment overall and then each individual country drives its own national sentiment with announcements – say of base rate movements, inflation figures or election news.

Global risk sentiment is normally a stronger driver, and a clearer indicator, of where the market is going than national risk sentiment.

Outcomes of sentiment: The Risk ON and Risk OFF indicators

There are five 'headline' clues in the market that we can look at which tell us whether the humans are risk ON or risk OFF. They are:

a) The US dollar: if the US dollar is rising the market overall is risk ON

b) If equities are rising then that's a sign that the market is risk ON as people move their money from bonds (fixed interest) to shares, that buying pushes up demand and prices rise, and which then also affects...

c) Bond yields: and we look at the US 10 year yield as a marker.

United States 10-Year Bond Yield

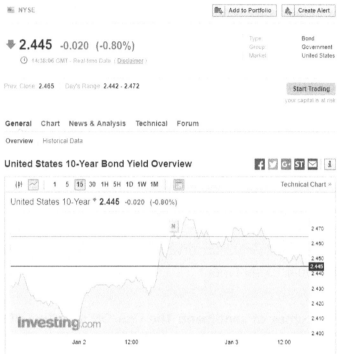

As people sell bonds, demand drops and so does the price of the bond, then the yield automatically rises. That is purely a mathematical consequence because the yield is calculated from the price and the interest paid, so as the price drops, the yield rises and this indicates that the market is risk ON.

N.B. The chart above would suggest that the market has gone risk OFF – the bond yield is dropping, suggesting that the price is rising.

d) Gold: as with bonds, people see gold as a secure, cautious investment and as people get more confident and risk ON, they sell their gold to buy shares, so the gold price falls. Then when people lose confidence they sell shares and buy gold – that is risk OFF

e)   Japanese yen also falls when the market is risk on and that's partly because people sell the yen to buy US dollars. There are other reasons for this movement which we don't need to learn at this stage.

The chart below summarises those outcomes, and of course all the signs and indicators are reversed if the market is risk OFF.

Sentiment

	Risk on	Risk off
USD	Rise	Fall
US 10 Year yield	Rise	Fall
Equities	Rise	Fall
JPY	Fall	Rise
GOLD	Fall	Rise

Fundamentals + Sentiment

In trading we use national and global fundamentals *added* to national and global sentiment as strong indicators.

The best trades, and those likely to have more chance of success, are when the fundamentals and the sentiment agree, so we look for both being aligned and in the same direction. We are specifically looking for when the sentiment endorses or confirms the fundamentals. They can agree in either direction – up or down – to create a strong trade.

Technicals

With trading, when we are aware that the Fundamentals and the Sentiment are in alignment then we look for a technical sign on the price movement chart of one of our watch lists (the main indices, currencies and commodities), to confirm the potential, predicted price movement.

A technical sign comes from how the price of anything moves and it displays in certain formations and trends on the price movement chart. That's the next learning.

DAILY DIARY

Gill: It always amazes me how easy stuff becomes when you get into it and start unravelling the apparent complexities. I particularly like it if I can create a tick sheet or criteria list or spreadsheet to guide me, as all I have to do then is get enough ticks in enough boxes to start a trade.

I'm also surprised by how little you actually need to know in order to be so far ahead of everyone else!

Fear of the new or unknown tends to put us off learning stuff but I remember reading about Einstein once and he said he wasn't very bright but he just had the ability to stick with problems slightly longer than most people – and that's it!

Success is purely patience and tenacity. Successful people, good traders and investors aren't geniuses – they're just prepared to slog a little bit longer and push a little bit further, to get to that elusive place – which is only half a step in front of everyone else!

Michael: Now I know what everything means, and I've been looking at more charts and figures, it amazes me how much people's opinions can affect prices. This emphasises how little the general public know about trading but shows why we, as traders, must keep up to date with sentiment.

Week Twenty-Eight: 6th – 12th November 2017

LESSONS and LEARNINGS

We're now two thirds through the basic learnings of what impacts a trade. The three things are:

- Fundamentals
- Sentiment and
- Technicals.

With trading, when we are aware that the Fundamentals and the Sentiment are in line we can look for a technical sign on the price movement chart of one of our watch lists (the main indices, currencies and commodities) to see if there's a potential trade to do.

Technicals

A technical sign comes from how the price of anything moves and it displays in certain formations and trends on the price movement chart.

When we look at the price of anything in chart form we can normally see a line going from the bottom left corner to the top right corner as the price increases over time.

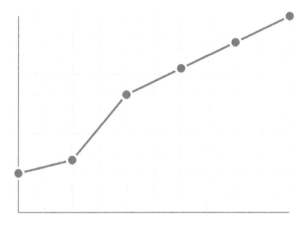

This bland generic chart could be anything and it would quite reasonably represent either house prices or share prices because broadly they have both moved up over many decades in a similar way.

As the chart gets more detailed and short-term, that trend line generally contains more wobbles and ups and downs that are normally lost in the big picture perspective of the longer term chart.

However, with most investment vehicles there is a limit to how detailed – or short-term – a chart can be. If we look at house prices in the UK for instance, we know that a house takes about 4 or 5 months to sell and therefore its price is only completely accurate at that one date of sale. Also, although there are a lot of property transactions per day the total number of property transactions each month in the UK is approximately 100,000 – so possibly 5,000 confirmed transactions per business day. Within those 5,000 transactions there are many different kinds of property – apartments, houses, leaseholds, freeholds, mansions and maisonettes – and so getting an accurate real price of any one type of property on any one day is incredibly difficult, because the amount of potential data we have is quite limited.

This isn't the same for currency, shares or commodities where there are millions of transactions per day, hour and minute. There are an estimated 1 million share transactions PER DAY in the UK: approximately $800 million in currency trades per day and somewhere near $13 billion in commodity trades.

That's a lot of trades.

As a consequence, it is very easy to map or chart the exact price of any share, group of shares (index), commodity or currency with absolute precision at any one time. We can easily find an accurate price and the larger the volume of trades the more accurate a price is because the sheer volume evens out all the extreme prices, and takes away any sense of guesswork.

And that's all a chart is – a map of all the different prices (grouped together as there are so many) at any time and the chart can be set to give prices at any time interval from one minute to one month – or longer.

Here's an example of the FTSE 100 index: over a couple of months with the prices calculated daily:

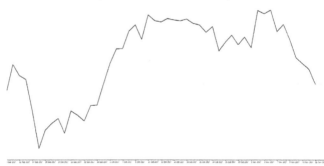

Now we also have the option of looking at that chart in a variety of ways and one way is to see all the movements in a line as it is above or in blocks as shown below – and these are known as candlesticks.

Here's the same chart presented that way – with candlesticks:

There are some obvious things to see; some candlesticks are black when the price went DOWN that day and some are white when the price went UP. These colours are arbitrary and could be anything but in general they are black or red if the price goes down that day and white or green if the price goes up.

There are also some sticks up and down which give us information:

Therefore, we can see how a price has moved in a day and by how much. If a candlestick is moving up the open price will be lower than the close price as it has risen throughout the period. Then, if a candlestick is going down the opening price will be higher than the close price.

N.B. A price does NOT have to open on one day in the same place, or at the same price as it closed the day before!

We can also see if all four prices (the open, close, high and low) are close together, which would tend to indicate that the price is fairly solid and that the market feels it is pretty accurate.

Or, if the four prices vary widely we can assume that there is some testing of the price because traders don't feel it's accurate – or it could be that the price is more volatile.

If we watch these charts over time, we start to see trends from which we can make predictions. Simplistically, charts where the bars close higher each day is an indicator of an upward price trend, and likewise, a down trend is easily spotted from lower closing prices.

Of course, it's far more complicated than that in daily reality but broadly, that's what the charts are showing us on a daily basis.

We can also extrapolate longer term trends where we can identify the prices moving in blocks, or waves. We can also identify the average prices over different periods of time, and the volume traded. All of these things are indicators from which we can make predictions of the next price movement – and that's where our trades emerge.

The more accurate the prediction, the better the trade.

Week Twenty-Nine: 13th – 19th November 2017

LESSONS and LEARNINGS

We're almost there now with the basic learnings of what impacts a trade. The three things are:

- Fundamentals
- Sentiment and
- Technicals.

Technicals

I know that I can glean a lot from watching and analysing the regular movements of the price of anything on a chart. This is done with trends, candlesticks and all manner of statistical tools.

However, we can also get an idea of where a price is going from a slightly bigger perspective picture of price movements, and we can start that learning by looking at channelling.

We have below a daily chart showing a share price fluctuating between two points: a high point and a low point.

It seems that the price just won't go above the high point and as soon as it gets near it does an about turn to start going down again because buyers will no longer buy at the high point price – or above it. That high point is known as **resistance.**

Likewise, as it goes down it seems that it just won't go below a certain low point and once again, it does an about turn when it gets there – that's known as **support.** It's the price at which the price is always supported because that's the level at which the sellers won't sell as the price it's too low.

These high and low points create a channel that the price just bounces between – and in an ideal world we could trade any given share or index or commodity as it does that.

What we would do is to buy it at the low point and sell at the high point over and over again, and trade into the sunset.

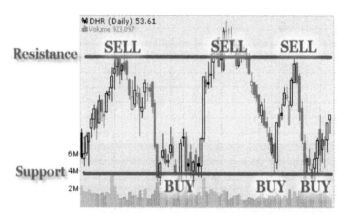

BUT it doesn't always work like that. It is very rare that a channel is distinctly clear and there's often a doubt as to whether the price is **exactly** at the low or the high and so there is an element of guesswork to it.

Also, channels don't always necessarily bounce around on this completely linear way and some channels go on an up trend trajectory (see the CISCO chart below) and some on a downwards one, and that also blurs the lines a little.

There are however many websites that will provide you with channelling stock information – see the list below. They tend to charge a monthly fee of about $10 per month and it's much more common to get recommendations on US shares than UK ones.

https://www.channelingstocks.com/
https://thestockbandit.com/channeling-stock/
http://wavestocks.com/

The element of guesswork however does take some of the juice or profit out of the deal. In order to be certain that the price **has** hit the bottom or the top you tend to have to wait for a strong indication that the price has really turned, and that wait reduces the return on what can be a tight profit expectation.

Let's look at a specific example here of the Bemis share price and on the side there is the channelling information.

The support price is identified at $21.60, and the resistance at $25.50.

It would be very unlikely that the price moved exactly at those points and so most traders would leave a 5% - 10% "turn" margin just to be certain.

This means that we would buy it after it hit the $21.60 support line and had moved up a bit just to make sure it was on its way up to resistance again.

Our buy price then would be about $21.60 + 5% - 10% i.e. about $22.75 - $23.

Likewise, our sell price would be at about $25.50 but it's most likely we would watch it come off that price and start to go down – and we would wait a short while to make sure it WAS going down and so our sell price would be: $25.50 – 5% - 10% i.e. about $22.75 - $23!

Mmmmm – that doesn't really work then does it as we don't make any profit from that!

In some cases it does work and if you get really good at channelling it can be a great strategy on its own, but for me I think channelling can be used more effectively as an indicator of a trade rather than a trade on its own.
And we can trade from:

- Bounces – as is normal with a channel
- Breakouts – from the channel
- New Highs – above resistance
- New Lows – below support

Here is the S&P 500 from May 2017 – and the star marks the point when the price breaks through the normal resistance line (highlighted). Once the resistance line is breached – the price then keeps moving up – and the breach is an indicator of a new price movement and a potential trade.

Breakout up through resistence

Breakout down through support

This is a chart of the Japan 225 in April 2017

There are two points to note: firstly, the channel itself is a bit 'wobbly' and not exact, so the highlighted section broadly shows us where it is.

Then there is a break out through the support and the price goes down.

Even if the price is not exactly in a clear channel we can still watch for new lows and new highs which give us an indication of where the price is going.

Illustration: new low: GB Index Oct 2016

Here is a new low

Illustration: New high: FTSE 250 Index February 2017

Here is a new high

Summary

There is much still to learn about how a price moves but channels and their associated movements are one of the technical indicators we need to watch, and it looks logical to me. I can see the patterns – all we need to do now is to learn how to trade them!

DAILY DIARY

Gill: Well, it's now December and as far as I'm concerned it is Christmas and I'm on holiday!
I also read that the forex market in particular gets very sluggish from the middle of December so it's not an ideal time to trade in any case.
I will check my portfolio from time to time but that's safely invested and I can leave it alone and I'm then perfectly poised for a launch of my trading activities in January 2018.

Michael: Channelling on its own is a really attractive prospect and I wanted to try it, but after a month of only just breaking even, it showed me how important it was to look at the technicals together with the fundamentals and sentiment.

Week Thirty: 20th – 26th November 2017

LESSONS and LEARNINGS: Tier Four

Trading Plan: Part one

There are many differences between the investing we've done at the lower Tiers of our Pyramid and the trading we're about to start.

1) Timing: there are two issues here – timing the market and time IN the market.

We never try to time the market with investing: the specific time we invest is irrelevant as the strategies are so long term that the market will certainly have ups, down, wobbles and stagnations many times in between when we buy and when we eventually sell. If we're expecting the market to rise by 10% per year, then the fact that one share might be one or two cents or pence higher at a certain time than another doesn't really add anything to our investing.

Whereas with trading it DOES matter. We're likely to be in the trade for only a few days and consequently, these smaller movements do count towards the eventual gain, so to get the exact right price, and a price that is one or two cents or pence better, for the trade is important.

Timing the entry points – timing the market is irrelevant for investing and vital for trading.

Time IN the market is also different. With investing it's the very long term: years, even decades. With trading it's going to be days or possibly weeks but it's unlikely to be longer than that.

2) This timing/time in principle continues for placing the orders; with investing we can take market orders and just take the price offered. With trading however, we're more likely to set our own price for the entry point and that's known as a limit order.

3) Connected to the orders is the broker and the transaction fees; with investing we need a standard share broker who charges us a transaction fee, with investing we need a specialist broker where we trade with no fees – apparently. With specialist brokers there is a very, very small difference between a buy and a sell price at any time which the broker takes as a 'turn' but it's minute and not going to affect our trading outcomes.

4) Trades: investing is in shares and a standard index, generally from the country where you reside. Trading can be with anything and anywhere globally. It can be with shares but is more likely to be with indices, currency (forex) or commodities like oil or gold.

5) What you transact changes: with investing you buy and sell a share or a unit and the price changes in

monetary amounts: cents or pence. With trading you buy a lot and the price changes in PIPs.

6) The stake in the deal varies. With investing we effectively go 'all in' and invest whatever we have as a 'lump sum' in the 'Dogs' strategy for instance, and put all our allocated monthly amount in a regular scheme for a tracker fund. With investing we use only a small proportion of our capital at any one time and this can be as small as 0.5% of our pot of money.

7) Capital preservation: although our first rule of investing or trading is to always preserve our capital, this is done differently for each approach. With investing we need to monitor our capital and watch it but there are bound to be times when our capital value drops. This is not a signal to sell but more of a signal to keep a closer eye for a while to see what's happening. We also know from our cost averaging exercise that with investing-type strategies a low price might be the opportunity to buy more and average down our overall cost of purchase.

That is NOT the case with trading. If the price goes away from you then that is normally the time to get out of the trade!

8) We would probably get out of the trade with a stop loss which would have been placed either automatically or manually when we enter a trade. This means that we put a reverse trade order in place to get out of the deal if the trade doesn't go as we hope. This limits the amount of money we can lose and stops the trade quickly: a stop loss. This isn't a relevant issue with

investing, especially at the bottom Two Tiers.

9) Trade variations: with investing there is really only one type of trade – you buy something and then eventually sell it. With trading we can also buy and then sell but we can also sell and then buy which is an odd concept for many. Buying first is called going *long* and selling first is called going **short**.

To explain that more, let's say I live in a town where there's a furniture store and I know the owner. I often go in there and I know what items there are for sale and I know there's a table in there for £500. I then happen to meet an old acquaintance in a pub and get chatting to them. She tells me that's she's refurbishing an old house and needs furniture. I ask her specifically what she wants and she says "I need a table". I describe the table I know is in the shop for £500 and offer to get her a table for £600.

She accepts, and I take her money. I then go back to the store and buy the table for £500: deliver it to her and I've made £100 by going 'short': selling the item before I actually bought it.

Now obviously it doesn't quite work like that with what we're trading but the principle is the same. You CAN sell before you buy.

10) Planning is also different. With investing it's a very broad plan to make 10% per year over a long period and although we may set a slightly different return and a varying length of time, that's the plan!

With trading there's a detailed weekly plan monitoring the fundamentals, the sentiment and the technicals of the dashboard items we're going to review. We also need to clearly define and plan our business objectives and control of risk.

And we will now look at that planning in more detail.

Daily Diary

Gill: Getting the difference between investing and trading very clear helps to get a much better focus on the trading activity. By clearly understanding investing, what it does and how we work with it helps to grasp, what NOT to do for trading.

Michael: In my opinion, the main difference between investing and trading is time investment. Trading isn't more difficult, it just takes more getting used to.

Week Thirty-One: 27th November – 3rd December 2017

LESSONS and LEARNINGS

In preparation for trading at Tiers Four and Five, I have now opened another broker account.

The standard broker accounts that we use for investing purposes are generalist, simple and cheap, and deal mainly in shares. For trading purposes we need a broker that deals in charts, currencies, indices, commodities and shares. They are unlikely to be the same broker.

I researched and found one that works for all the things we want it to do in the UK – and that's Fxpro: www.fxpro.co.uk

It's very easy, as before, to open both a dummy account and a live one (as long as you don't confuse the two). The dummy account can be opened in the blink of an eye and the real live account needs some identification checks and of course, some money.

It was relatively painless – and if you want to follow me there the things to note are:

Click FCA on the opening screen: I have put in a leverage of 1:500, and I chose to trade in GB£.

Other than that all the questions were personal – and I knew the answers to those!

179

I now have sitting on my desktop an Fxpro logo – with a demo account in it.

Other Territories

Fxpro does not operate globally so they may not be available to you. Just insert 'fx currency brokers' into a search engine and see what comes up. Although they are called currency brokers they should all cover shares, indices and commodities as well.

We need one that trades using MT4 (MetaTrader 4) and a leverage of 1:500 and then everything else should be the same. Although we set the leverage at 500 (which is generally the highest it can be), we do NOT want to actually trade at that level of leverage and we will cover that more later. There are indications that the UK government are going to restrict leverage to 1:10 for standard retail customers like us in the future. This is fine for the strategies we intend to trade, therefore any leverage set by your particular broker will be fine for our purposes.

MT4 (MetaTrader 4)

MT4 is the main trading platform that is used worldwide particularly for currency trading. You do not need to buy it as it is purchased by all the worlds brokers and they provide it free on all broker accounts. It is the common transaction method and the common 'language' of traders.

What to trade?

There are a couple of ideas: firstly, we don't want to be too risky – even though we're at Tier Four of the Pyramid and officially at the regular trading rather than the long-term investing end of the scale – we still need to be careful. Also, we should stick to stuff we broadly know.

Most of us 'know' a few currencies: sterling of course, the dollar and the euro are ones I'm familiar with and have had in my purse from time to time, and because of that I have a sense of their value and what they are worth to me. I can vaguely remember £1 being worth $2 and yet I know (from all the BREXIT press coverage) that £1 will now only buy me about $1.30. So, the pound is now worth less against the dollar than once it was.

Similarly with the euro: my vague sense is that once upon a time I could buy a euro for about £0.60 and I see today that I can buy a euro for nearer £0.90 – again, the pound is worth less.

And that seems a good enough sense of three major currencies to enable me to start with those – and the currency pairs that can be traded, which are:

GBPUSD

USDEUR

EURUSD

And as a result of me reading around this topic I get the sense that the Japanese yen is always in the mix – so I'm going to add that into my listing of pairs:

GBPJPY

EURJPY

USDJPY

That gives me 6 possible currency pairs to trade and that's enough. We don't want to have to know about currencies – nor their countries political or economic situation. I don't want to be watching this other than for 15 minutes at one end of the day or another.

You will note that each currency has its own three digit code which is fairly obvious.

Then secondly, we know a bit about shares or equities and indices – as we've traded those before in Tier One: The Cappuccino Factor strategy, and using just that glimmer of knowledge and my currency selections we can watch and potentially trade: the indices from Europe (Germany and the EU seem to have indices), the UK and the US and possibly Japan.

They also fit my *'only trade indices if the stock market is north of the Equator'* rule that I established back at Tiers One and Two. If I include all the permutations of those, I come up with 10 potential trades or charts to watch on fxpro, and I've added purely for completeness, Goldoz and WTI (oil) because they are the two important commodities and economic markers.

We can also add the Australia Index although that breaks the north of the Equator rule – so that we can test that rule using just one market.

That gives us the 12 potential things to trade and we'll set up a monitoring system on our MT4 platform for those later.

The next step is to load up the broker account and then watch, and understand, a trade.

Tick Tock Time Tip!

Well, the clocks went back in the UK this week so I was keen to see if the time had changed on my fxpro account – and it didn't! As usual, the server time was exactly 2 hours ahead of UK time. I can't say I understand that but I reckon it's because the server is based somewhere that's always 2 hours ahead – but frankly, it doesn't matter if that's right or not as long as I always remember the two hour ahead rule.

Most of the time it doesn't matter – the currency markets are open from 10 p.m. on a Sunday night until 10 p.m. on a Friday night – so there is no 'open and close' to worry about.

But time can be important for equity trades – and the indices – because those markets do open and close at the start and end of the relevant country's stock market day. We know that stock prices can move at those times and occasionally gap up or down when the markets open. That creates a slight challenge for us, so it's best avoided.

Therefore, I've checked the open and close times of each main market – as they **impact the fxpro account** – which is the important thing here. I need to monitor the open and close on the account itself, and the timings are:

UK	07:00 – 21:00
USA	07:00 – 21:00
Germany	07:00 – 21:00
Australia	01:00 – 21:00
Japan	01:00 – 21:00

I reckon the best time to trade then is in the evenings UK time – and before 21.00, and before 16.00 in the USA.

Daily Diary

Gill: Trading seems a real and exciting possibility now I have my trading account open. I feel like an experienced trader.

Michael: Ironically, for this supposedly more difficult trading, this step was much easier. The broker probably only took a couple of hours to set up, and I was able to set up some friends account's on the same day. There are also fewer charts to look at which is helpful. Their movements also look fairly predictable.

Merry Christmas
We are taking a break, see you in the new year.

Week Thirty-Seven: 8th – 14th January 2018

LESSONS and LEARNINGS: Tier Four

FXPRO: MT4

At the moment we just want to feel comfortable and confident that we can open charts and set up some base line information so, I'm going to set up a standard set or blocks of accounts: that will include all the basic equity indices. These are the 12 potential charts or trades that we have already identified.

FXPRO:MT4

The MT4 screen can look a bit complicated but the more you click around the more comfortable it becomes.

All brokers also have a variety of demonstration videos and downloads to help with familiarisation. If you get stuck just go back to a completely blank screen and start again.

My account is not actually trading so it shows only the £50,000 'demo' money I requested when I set up the account and as a complete beginning to the broker screens, it will look like, or similar to, this:

Then the first thing I want to see is the control information on the left-hand side and I want to see Market Watch (which is the list of all the possible things I can watch or trade in the Market), the Navigator (which shows me all the details about my account and what indicators I have set and so on) and the Data Window (which shows me the prices of the trade I'm looking at and the figures flick up and down all the time as you place your mouse over a chart.

I click on VIEW on the tool bar and those three items are on the drop down menu so I click on those:

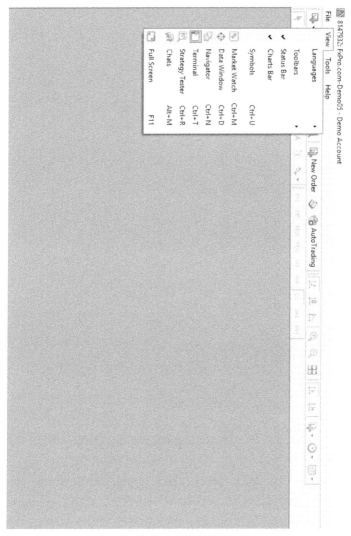

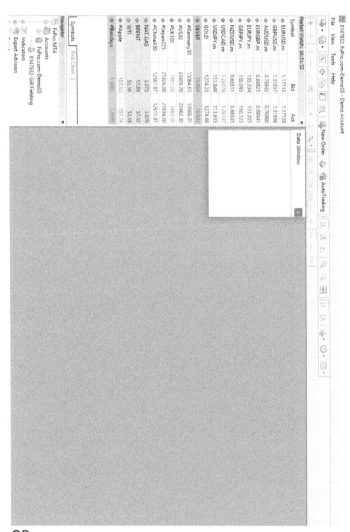

OR

I can do (Ctrl + M) for Market Watch, Control N for the Navigator and Control D for the Data Window.

Now, if your Data Window turns up somewhere you don't want it (like above) – and I prefer it on the left-hand side with all the other core information - then all you do is drag and drop it to where you want. All you need to do is click on the top header part of the Data Window and then move the mouse to take it wherever you want.

You may also want to resize the boxes (just hover over the upper or lower edge until you get the double arrow and then expand or contract the box) – until you getting it looking exactly as you like it. Here's mine:

www.financialinvestingandtrading.com

Loading a chart

Now I have the blank set up I can load and delete charts at will.

To open any chart I can either click on the green plus sign OR the arrow next to it at the top left on the toolbar and a list of main charts will appear:

www.financialinvestingandtrading.com

A drop down menu will then appear listing all the major charts, plus groups of 'forex majors' and 'spot indices' and we can then go to sub menus and look for what we want.

If you don't get a drop down list just hover over the white header column in the market watch box – marked symbol - Bid - Ask and then right click and you then get an option to 'show all' – click that and you will then have a complete list of every possible chart. You can also do the same and say 'hide all' if you're fed up with the list.

Once you have a list then choose a chart to practice with and either right click and click on chart window, or you can just drag and drop a chart from the list onto the grey space, and your chart will appear.

N.B. if you drag and drop a second chart into the chart window it will overwrite the first one, so make sure you drag and drop it into a different place in the window. If you open chart window the system will automatically place each chart in a slightly different place.

For now, we just need one chart to look at and I have GBPUSD.

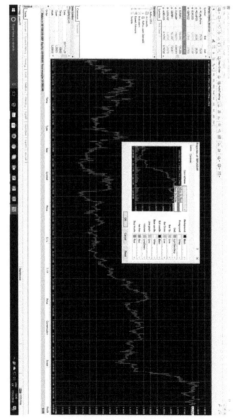

www.financialinvestingandtrading.com

I have now clicked on the Chart then properties from the top tool bar and I have this screen. I can also get to this screen by pressing F8.

The system defaults to a green on black screen but set the colour scheme to suit you and then also set the bars and lines (the right-hand list of options) to whatever colour scheme you fancy.

If in any doubt at this stage just leave it all at the default setting and change it later when you have more of an idea of what how you want to review your charts.

Then you can choose whether to have the grid lines on the chart – they're quite useful to measure or gauge rises and falls but I know some people find them annoying – and you click on charts grid and the grid lines will disappear and then just do that again and they will reappear.

Again, I'm just going to leave it all as default set up for now.

Finally, on the chart we will immediately see prices – in the top left corner of the chart itself there are the current prices and they will be moving and then there will be a white line across the chart ending in a highlighted number on the right-hand side, which shows us where the current trade price is.

As an exercise, load up a chart and flick around on it. If it disappears, don't worry just reload it and start again! This is a demo account and you won't break it.

Daily Diary

Gill: The more I click, flick and drag with these charts and accounts, the more familiar I am with it and the more fun it seems. What started off as being completely alien and scary has now become a reassuring sight, and the education sessions on the broker's own website have been helpful.

However, in all honesty, it's better to just click and flick about yourself to see what happens!

Michael: This is the same as all broker accounts, you need to setup a demo account to get to know the platform. Luckily, it is very easy to do on Fxpro and you can set up as many accounts as you want. I would recommend just playing around on a demo account as it's the quickest way to learn.

Week Thirty-Eight: 15th – 21st January 2018

LESSONS and LEARNINGS: Tier Four

FXPRO: MT4 Part Two

At this stage I can also change the appearance of the charts and get them working as I need.

The toolbar along the top gives us all the options we need:

We will cover them all in time but let's start with the first block on the middle left:

Moving from the left: the first icon, with the cross, will open a dropdown menu of charts to load; the second icon is for profiles (see later in this session); the next three are Market Watch, Data Window and Navigator – all of which we need for our trading.

The next button along is a square, whitish button which turns on the terminal display or turns it off. The terminal is the section at the bottom – if you look closely the word is written sideways on the left-hand side in grey. The terminal contains all the accounting, communication and administrative information for your account. I like to keep mine visible so I can see how much money I have available at any time, but if you remove that display it does allow more space to enlarge the chart.

The next three buttons are for strategy testing information to be collated (and we don't have any of that yet); to click to place a trade or order (which we will look at in greater detail later) and finally, to turn on auto trading. We don't have auto trading and this is normally for 'robot' systems. If the blob at the bottom of the auto trading button is red the auto trader is turned off.

The next group of buttons are mainly about **chart presentation:**

The first three buttons on the left give us the option to see our information in bars:

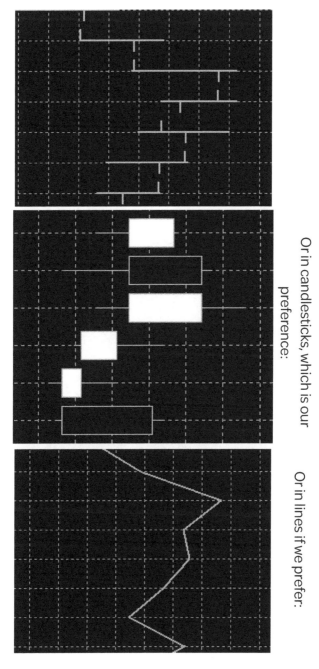

Or in candlesticks, which is our preference:

Or in lines if we prefer:

Then there are the zoom in and out buttons, followed by the tile button. The tile button is useful when we have many charts, as it allows us to see all the charts on one screen rather than having to flick from one to the other. If we had 6 charts that we wanted to monitor we can load them, up click on the tiles button and they would then be displayed like this:

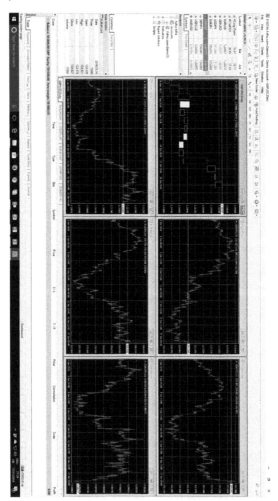

www.financialinvestingandtrading.com

The next two buttons move the chart to the end – or most recent candlestick and the second of those moves the chart information slightly to the left so that there's space on the right, which is helpful if you're drawing lines to see where you think the price will go.

The next button (also has a green cross) gives us a list of potential indicators, and we will load some shortly. The indicators are also listed in the navigator box on the left.

The next button (which looks like a clock) allows us to set the period covered by each bar or candle and that can also be set by clicking on the time buttons on the lower toolbar:

M1	M5	M15	M30	H1	H4	D1	W1	MN

Time periods are:

M1	One minute
M5	Five minutes
M15	Fifteen minutes
M30	Thirty minutes
H1	One hour
H4	Four hours
D1	One day
W1	One week
M1	One month

And that means that the candle displays information about the prices: open, close, high and low for that particular time period. For now we will set our time period as daily D1, so we get one candle per day to analyse.

The final button on that toolbar allows us to save our preferences!

So set the chart to look how you want: set the colours, the period, the grid, whatever you like and once you are happy with that save your preferences in a template by clicking on that last button: you can save your preferences as a template and name it whatever you like but if you save your template as **default.tpl** that format and template will be used every time you load a chart.

The Dashboard

We can now set up a dashboard of the key charts to monitor and watch, which we can do that with a **dashboard** and we can load that in every time we start to look at trading anything, to give a bigger perspective of what's going on globally. This will provide the strategic view.

Using our potential trades list from an earlier session we can set up our personal dashboard. They are:

#US$index_27
#USSPX500
#US30
#USNDAQ100
#UK100
#UK_Mid250
#Euro50
#Germany30
#Japan225
#Aus200
WTI
GOLDoz

To find those I just scroll down the list in market watch until I see the one I want and then right click on that to load it:

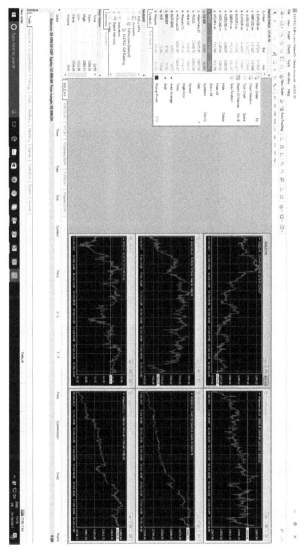

Then once you have all the 12 charts loaded, click on the tile button.

And your dashboard will appear like this:

When you're happy with the monitoring chart list you can save that as a profile:

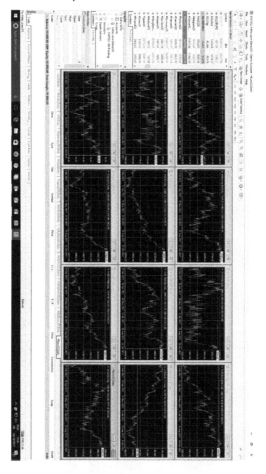

Click on file: profiles, save as and that will bring up a box and you can call that group of accounts what you like – I'm going to use Dashboard.

www.financialinvestingandtrading.com

That then gives us our list of initial charts to use as guidance – we can quickly flick through all those charts to give us a sense of what the market is doing before we look at anything specific.

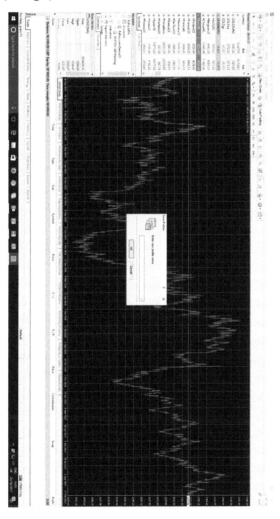

Now whenever I log on to my account I can bring up my basic dozen dashboard charts very easily. Click on file

- profiles and dashboard will appear as a possible – click on that and the 12 charts will appear.

Daily Diary

Gill: I like having a dashboard of charts to look at to give me a sense of familiarity when I first open the account and before I look at anything new. I can look at those to see what's happening on charts I'm familiar with and that gives me a grounding, and a sense of comfort before I explore new information.

Michael: I have been surprised by how easy it has been to pick up the MT4 platform. Compared to other platforms I've used so far this is the most intuitive. If profiles and templates are troubling you don't worry, at the end of the day the most important things are that you can see the charts of what you want and that you can place trades on them.

Week Thirty-Nine: 22nd – 28th January 2018

LESSONS and LEARNINGS: Tier Four

Starting to Trade: The PIPs, Points and Prices!

With individual shares it's easy to understand the how we transact. We transact in shares and we pay money: pennies, dollars or whatever. With trading however we trade in PIPS and POINTS, LOTS and CONTRACTS!

Currency: PIPs and Lots

Each currency has a three letter code, and our main eight currencies to trade are:

GBP	Great Britain Pound
USD	USA Dollars
EUR	Euro
JPY	Japanese Yen
AUD	Australian Dollar
NZD	New Zealand Dollar
CAD	Canadian Dollar
CHF	Swiss Franc

If we trade currency the deal is reported in currency pairs so GBPUSD means buying Great Britain Pounds with USA dollars: The first currency code listed is the one being bought by the second currency listed.

The price of GBPUSD will look like this:

GBPUSD 1.29389.

That Fourth decimal place is the PIP - the actual UNIT that we trade - and the PIP is just a general trading unit used for all currencies. A PIP is the smallest incremental amount a currency can move and it stands for Price Interest Point.

Be careful here as the main currencies (excluding Japan see below) price to FIVE decimal places but it's the Fourth decimal place that we're interested in for trading.

N.B. With JPY it's the second decimal point that counts in the trade (because there are just so many yen to every other currency):

USDJPY 113.234.

We can broadly estimate that a PIP is worth about $10. It changes of course but broadly today a PIP is worth $10 on currency pairs including the USD, slightly less for currency pairs including the yen and slightly more if the pair includes the euro. This doesn't really matter as we will check the exact price for each trade, but it gives us an approximate guide.

When trading currency the price is in PIPs and the quantity traded is a LOT or part LOT and we can trade anything from 0.01 of a lot.

One lot is 100,000 currency units of the first currency in the pair.

Indices: Points and Contacts

An index or indices are transacted in POINTS, and when an index is reported:

FTSE 7779.87.

The point is the single unit: the 7779.87.

If the index moves by 10 points it would become 7789.87.

We trade in quantities known as contracts, and again, we can trade small amounts in part contracts.

Exceptions

Overall, with our trading we are likely to be looking at a restricted number of possibilities – certainly in the beginning. These will be the main equity indices (our dashboard list); then potentially 6 currency pairs (EURUSD, GBPUSD, USDJPY, EURJPY, EURGBP and GBPJPY) and we will also keep an eye on gold and oil.

They both trade in points and contracts as for the equity indices, but with oil – if we take WTI (West Texas Intermediate) which is a good barometer of oil prices – we trade in not ONE contract but ONE THOUSAND contracts.

With Gold there are different types of gold trade and if we stick to trading Goldoz (ounces) then we trade in one contract at a time but the standard Gold (just listed as Gold and not Goldoz – be careful when you select the chart) then we trade in ONE HUNDRED contracts.

Summary

Although that feels like a lot of information, it is all quite simple when we start trading because the MT4 system does much of the work and automatically sets the deal parameters in lots and contracts as part of the order.

And the summary is this:

- Currency pairs are priced in PIPs (the 4th decimal place in the price) and traded in Lots or part Lots.
  - Except Japanese yen which is in PIPs (the second decimal place in the price – and this will be obvious because there isn't a fourth decimal place in a JPY price!).
- Equity Indices and Goldoz are priced in points (the single unit digit in the price) and traded in contracts or part contracts.
  - Except WTI which is traded in 1,000 contracts.

And that's it!

Examples: £ $

1) Currency

Let's say we have a balance on our account of £50,000. We know from our plan and strategy (see later) we want to risk, and are prepared to lose, 0.5% of our money on a trade i.e. £250. We work out from looking at our chart that our stop loss is about 38 PIPs, so our potential loss is £250 divided by 38 = 6.58 PIPs per £.

We can then convert that into $ at say $1.3 to the £ to get our potential risk in PIPs per dollar: 6.58 * 1.3 = $8.55.

We know that trades are in Lots of approximately $10 per PIP.

Therefore, our trade size and our risk in this particular trade is:

$8.55/10 = 0.855 or rounded to 8.56.

2) Indices

Let's assume that rather than trading currency that we want to trade the USSPX500 (the US Standard and Poors 500 index), but we still only want to risk the same 0.5% so £250. We look at the chart and see that our stop loss position would be set at about 280 points.

We calculate the stop loss position to £ to be £250/280 i.e. 0.89 points per £: convert to US dollars as before at say 1.3 = 0.89 * 1.3 = $1.157 per point.

With indices the contracts are $1 per point.

Our trade size is therefore: 1.157/1 = 1.157 or rounded to 1.16 contracts.

There are several assumptions in these simple examples that we do not yet know: the risk, the stop loss, or in fact, the trade itself, and we will cover all of those shortly.

Daily Diary

Gill: With all of these things, the more you practice and flick about the easier the calculations become and in any case, we have a method to calculate all these lots and contracts sizes automatically – but it's always good to know how to create these numbers from scratch yourself – and that gives me comfort because it means I have the ability to check the automated calculations too!

Michael: I agree with my mum here, I don't think there is any easy way round this part, you just have to practice. If you are struggling with it, the maths isn't that hard, the jargon used in it is what really caused the confusion.

6. Tier Four - Part Two

Week Forty: 29th January – 4th February 2018

LESSONS and LEARNINGS: Tier Four

Indicators: The automated risk manager

Although we now know how to calculate a trade deal size and the risk attached to it – we have an easier way! We have developed (corporately that is) an automated risk manager which will do it all for you.

It can be loaded onto any MT4 trading platform as an indicator and when it is first loaded it will appear like this:

Fundamentally the only amendments we need on the risk manager are the inputs sheet.

IF we want to set our risk at 0.5% of our pot of money then we input 0.5 in the risk percentage space and then add in the price we want to enter the trade and the stop loss we require.

Let's say we are looking at a GBPUSD trade and we are going to enter the market at the current price of 1.3957 expecting the price to continue to rise and therefore setting our stop loss at 1.3856.

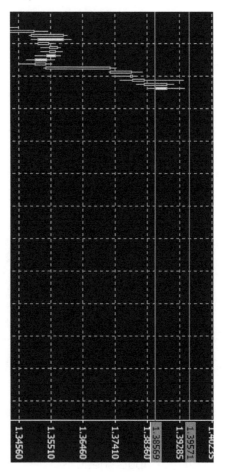

www.financialinvestingandtrading.com

To calculate the risk and lot size you can either:

- Calculate it manually, as we've seen in an earlier session

- Create a spreadsheet following the process in the manual session, and just multiply and divide as instructed there, or

- If you are interested in obtaining a copy of the automated risk manager go to this website:

www.fit/manager

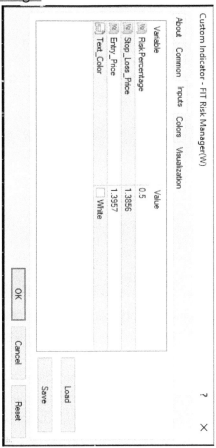

www.financialinvestingandtrading.com

If I complete the input sheet of the automated risk manager with those figures this is what I get:

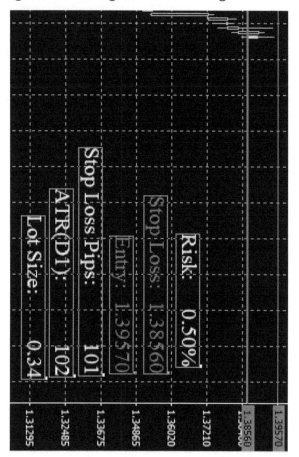

And then I click OK and the risk and figures now appear on my screen and it also gives me my lot size of 0.34 to trade.

All I need to do now – IF I were going to trade this – would be to click on F9 and the order box would appear. I transfer the figures from the risk manager onto the box and press submit and I would be in the trade.

Indicator: ATR: Average True Range

The ATR is a very useful indicator that we can load in at this stage. We can find it either in the indicators list in the navigator pane on the left or as one of the indicators in the drop down list on the toolbar (third from the right and has a green cross).

If you right click over the ATR line it will allow you to 'Attach to Chart' and when you do that an input screen appears:

The input screen is pre-set to 14 days and this means that the ATR will calculate the average daily price movement over the last 14 day period – so it gives you an indication of how much the price moves normally and on average per day. Some stocks and currencies move a lot more each day than others and this gives you some guidance as to what to expect.

This is incredibly helpful when setting a trade because if we know that a currency normally moves by say 25 PIPs as a daily average we need to set our stop loss based on that because if we set a stop loss of say 3 PIPs then we will be taken out of the trade just because of the normal behaviour and movement of the currency price.

The ATR gives you the average of the last 14 days, or the 14 days from where you are holding the cursor if you want to look at a 14 day period from the past.

I'm using 14 days as my input because that gives me about enough of a period to gauge the normal volatility, but we can also use longer periods in there and also compare say the 14 day average to longer averages. This allows us to get a sense of the price in the short term versus the longer term.

If we use our previous example of the GBPUSD, you will see that I have already loaded the ATR on that chart and it tells me that the average daily price movement is 102 PIPs and I've set my stop loss at about the same level in the expectation that I won't be taken out of this trade just on normal daily volatility.

That's NOT why I set the stop loss there – we will cover that in a later session – but it's a great tool and an added piece of information I use when deciding on my trade figures.

N.B. Both the automated risk manager and the ATR are indicators and if we load them onto one of our charts and we want to keep that as our default template, don't forget to save it as we go. A quick way of doing that is to hover on the chart itself, right click, select templates, save as and select either default or a new name as you wish.

Indicator: Moving averages

The other indicator that is very commonly used is the moving average button as this gives us a sense of where the price is going over different periods of time. Most people use these in pairs – a long term and a short-term and then see how the two compare. If the long term average price is higher than the short term price but the short term price average line is moving towards the long term line then we can make some assumptions about where the short term price is going to hit or stop moving. when the lines cross it indicates of a trend direction change.

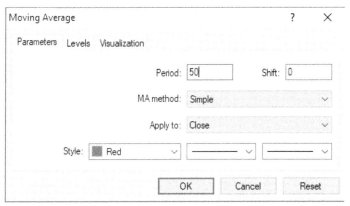

To load the moving average lines click on the moving average indicator in the navigator box: click Indicator:

Trend: Moving Average and then you will get an input box. Create two lines (of different colours!) and let's set up a 50 day and a 200 day moving average to give us some useful comparisons.

Moving average lines can also act as indicators of support and resistance.

Drawing Toolbar

The charts are now beginning to look familiar and contain useful information, and there is no real substitute for just clicking and playing with all the buttons on your demo account.

There are some functions we haven't yet discussed and that's the drawing set:

And they are from left to right:

The crosshairs – which places across on the chart

Line up and down (vertical)

Line side to side (horizontal)

Diagonal line

To use each of these just click on the symbol on the toolbar, then click on the chart (you will need to click and drag to make a diagonal line). Use these to identify lines of support, resistance, projected prices, stop losses and so on.

After that there is an equidistant channel function and this will enable to you to draw a channel on the chart to see if the price is bouncing between support and resistance or not.

This is incredibly useful as most of our trades will be looking at the support and resistance and break outs from those.

Next to that we have the Fibonacci retracement function which we will not use at the beginning of our trading but we will consider in a later session.

Finally, on the toolbar there are three buttons allowing us to draw textboxes, arrows, markers etc on our charts, and you will either completely ignore these or develop your own favourites as you go.

And that's it with MT4! We've now looked at every button and option, loaded some indicators and clicked about.

Daily Diary

Gill: It seems like a lot of things to look at but actually I don't look at many! Although the options are there I really only look at two or three things, and you will soon develop your own personal favourites.

Michael: The indicator that works best for you is very subjective. Some people really like visual information, so the moving averages will be more helpful. Whereas others may prefer numerical data so the ATR will be more useful. So test them out to see what works for you. Don't forget your broker will have more indicators than we've covered so check some of them out as well.

Week Forty-One: 5th – 11th February 2018

LESSONS and LEARNINGS: Tier Four

The Complete Trading Plan

We now know that there are many differences between investing and trading and we need to explore a few of those differences in order to place an actual trade.

It is always sensible to start with the top level:

The strategy.

With investing there is an expectation that eventually the shares will increase in value; with trading we have to accept that not every trade will win. That's a difficult concept to believe – before we even start – that we're going to get it wrong sometimes. But as long as we get more winners than losers then our trading is successful.

When trading, we cannot win all the time. The market does odd things and quickly, but if we understand that then the concept is incredibly liberating! We can accept that we cannot entirely read the market and that removes the pressure to always get it right.

Our business model needs to reflect that and we need to set a strategy where:

- We win more often than we lose on trades: say 60% win to 40% lose
- We win more than we lose in absolute terms and restrict our losses to say, 0.5% of our pot of money and we profit target 1% of our pot of money

As long as we always keep these ratios in our favour we will always profit overall and we can accept that we can sometimes lose and it still works.

And this is not at all dissimilar to the earlier strategies. When we invest in an index we don't expect that every single share in the index is rising – there will always be some shares going up and some going down. As I look at my UK 'Dogs' portfolio this morning I can see that in fact of the 10 shares 6 are up and 4 are down but overall they are up in total by 4.09%. A ratio of 60%/40% works perfectly well there and it will work perfectly well with trading at Tier Four.

The risk itself

The risk we take is very much a personal matter but in the early days I suggest we set it small. We know from our usual compounding knowledge that small amounts over time compound into huge amounts, and there is no need to abandon that principle now!

So start small. Set a limit on how much you are prepared to lose and risk on each trade – let's start with 0.5%.

Therefore, if your available pot of money is say, $500 then each trade should only risk 0.5% of that, i.e. $2.50. If your pot is £10,000 then each trade should risk £50.

	Price	Change	Change %	Value	Cost	Gain/Loss	Gain/Loss %
221 ASTRAZENECA ORD USD0.25	5,175.00p	17.66p	0.34%	£11,436.75	£10,132.34	£1,304.41	12.87%
2318 BP ORD USD0.25	526.90p	-0.31p	-0.06%	£12,213.54	£10,333.29	£1,880.25	18.20%
3374 BT GROUP ORD GBP0.05	271.30p	3.90p	1.46%	£9,153.66	£10,340.19	£-1,186.53	-11.47%
663 GLAXOSMITHKLINE ORD GBP0.25	1,351.60p	-3.32p	-0.25%	£8,961.11	£10,113.99	£-1,152.88	-11.40%
1360 HSBC HOLDINGS PLC ORD USD0.50	762.20p	4.33p	0.57%	£10,365.92	£10,188.83	£177.09	1.74%
292 IMPERIAL BRANDS PLC GBP0.10	3,166.00p	-1.33p	-0.04%	£9,244.72	£10,037.07	£-792.35	-7.89%
1061 NATIONAL GRID ORD GBP0.12431289	863.10p	-1.42p	-0.16%	£9,157.49	£9,997.25	£-839.76	-8.40%
471 ROYAL DUTCH SHELL 'A'SHS EUR0.07(GBP)	2,527.00p	4.45p	0.18%	£11,902.17	£9,980.75	£1,921.42	19.25%
481 ROYAL DUTCH SHELL 'B'ORD EUR0.07	2,566.00p	8.025p	0.31%	£12,342.46	£10,292.21	£2,050.25	19.92%
4522 VODAFONE GROUP ORD USD0.2095238	238.50p	1.025p	0.43%	£10,784.97	£9,998.43	£786.54	7.87%
				£105,562.79	£101,414.35	£4,148.44	4.09%

Then add to that a profit target and let's double that at say, 1%. We then know that if we gain twice what we lose and we win 60% of the time and lose on 40% then all the odds are in our favour.

And then keep the risk % constant over your balance. So, if you start with $500 and lose a trade and you lose $2.50 then your next risk is 0.5% of what you have left, which is $497.50, i.e. a risk of $2.49.

Likewise, if you win a trade then your balance goes up from $500 to $505 (1% gain) then next trade risks 0.5% of that, i.e. $2.53.

And even if your balance is quite large I would still start like this and then only change these risk figures when you have enough evidence – and if the system works for you then maybe never change them at all.

However, please keep accurate records of what you risk and lose and win and the percentages of win to lose trades because only then will any of these figures make sense and you can flex and adjust your proportions accordingly.

Back to the basics

We've come a long way since we looked at the basics of trading which was looking at the fundamentals, the sentiment and the technicals. The MT4 system and platform gives us the technical information well enough but how do we find out about the global fundamentals that we need to review?

Fortunately, somebody else does all the work. There are many websites that will give a global overview of all the major events and the expectation of what is going to happen.

One useful site is www.forexfactory.com and if you look at the weekly calendar you will see something like this:

The calendar tells us the significant events or announcements for each day. It highlights the country or currency concerned in our normal three digit code and it also ranks the items, and those items with a red square alongside are the most significant and the bright yellow are the least significant and the orange squares are in between. It's normally enough to look just at the red square items.

Then, on the right-hand side, the site will tell us the expectation of what is going to happen.

Next we should look at the GBP average earnings index. This highlights it as a significant event and tells us that the previous announcements was for a 2.5% growth and this time it's expected to be the same.

| GBP | | Average Earnings Index 3m/y | | | 2.5% | 2.5% |

For each week make a list of all the major items expected. There will be announcements affecting other items: stocks, indices etc, as well as just currencies.

Then, taking each of those announcements, go into a general search engine and financial news sites to see what the sentiment is attached to that particular currency or index or country.

This might not be entirely clear at first but what we are looking for is a movement in sentiment that endorses the fundamental news, as that gives the strongest trades.

It makes sense to create a sheet for each week to record and reflect – we can keep these for review as we go along.

In the next session we will take these pieces of information to guide us to particular trades to look at.

Daily Diary

Gill: This is all beginning to feel very real now and I can see a logical step by step process guiding me from a big general picture of the world to something very specific and tangible to trade.

Michael: Now we know what our plan is, everything that may change the price of a commodity or equity and we have the tools, we just need to do the research.

Week Forty-Two: 12th – 18th February 2018

LESSONS and LEARNINGS: Tier Four

The Complete Trading Plan: Part Two

We now have:

1) A strategy

2) A broad annual plan

3) A process of looking for weekly fundamentals endorsed by sentiment

We can now turn those general guides into specifics to create weekly watch plan sheet.

Illustration of a weekly plan

Let's say our review of the fundamentals and sentiment is that we expect equities to rise and, for instance, we expect the dollar to be strong. This could be because there's an announcement in the USA confirming tax advantages, which is driving the US stock market and in turn, that's pulling the UK market up with it. Added to that, let's say, the US federal reserve are hinting (and they always hint!) at increasing interest rates so that is moving the dollar up against other currencies.

(By the way, all those 'let's says' and 'for examples' in that last paragraph are all real events from the second half of 2017.)

From that knowledge we can compile a list of charts to look at and, for instance, we could choose:

a)   Any of the USD currency pairs

The currency pairs that are normally traded with USD in currency are USDJPY, GBPUSD and EURUSD.

Let's load up those charts but remember, we're expecting the USD to rise – so we will be looking for the USDJPY to go long (to buy) as it rises, and with the other two pairs the USD is the second currency so we are expecting the first currency to fall against the second (USD) and therefore we would need to go short (to sell) those two.

b)   Any of the US indices: S&P500, US30, USDAQ100 plus the UK100

That gives us a list of seven potential charts to look at and I suggest that on any given week we look at about 6 – 12 maximum, otherwise it gets too time intensive, and I've put them in tiles so I can see them all at once.

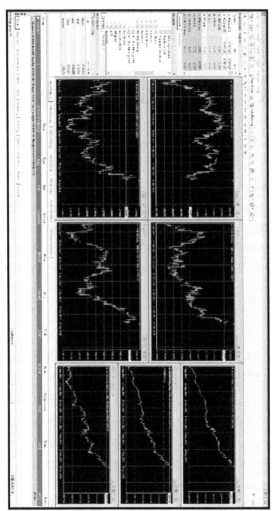

I would then save these 7 charts as a new profile to look at for this week.

File: profiles: save them as a new profile – WEEK ONE in this instance.

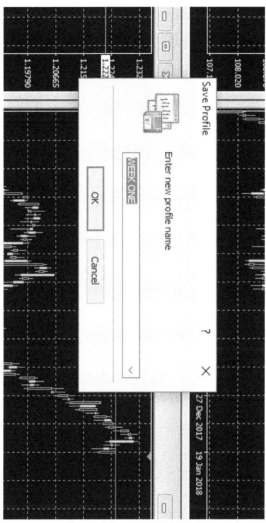

(You can see where this process is going and eventually we will have 52 weeks of profiles and records of what we were watching at any given week over a year, which we can then review and, with the benefit of hindsight, actually see where the trades went. This is the best and most accurate learning tool we have!)

When you save a profile you will see the name pop up at the very bottom of the screen:

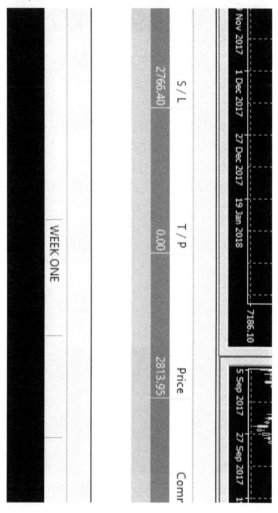

And then if you click on that you will see a list of all other profiles you have set up and at the moment we should just have our dashboard of charts we set up earlier and now our Week One charts.

Daily review

Now all we have to do is to review those charts to find a technical set up with our candlesticks that confirms or endorses our view.

We need to look for support and resistance, as always, and then look for a bounce away from one of those lines or a breakout from the channel or a new high or a new low and that, together with the indicators we've already set, should give us a trade for that week.

As an example, if we look at the USDJPY chart that I've loaded today (and therefore doesn't necessarily correlate to the fundamentals we've talked about earlier) we can see a very nice channel. I've marked the ceiling or resistance line at the top and used a shaded box where I perceive the channel to be:

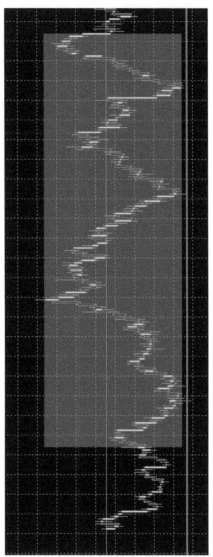

Now at the moment, the chart price is in between the support and resistance lines and my general expectation is that the price will go down to somewhere near the support line but as this price is floating about in the middle, this isn't a clear enough signal for a trade yet.

Then if we look at the US30 (the Dow Jones) we can see a relentless price line up over the past year so here we would be trading on the possibility of higher highs.

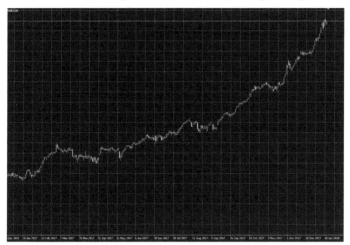

Summary

We can now summarise the key seven steps to trading:

1) Set a big strategy – say, to make 20% return on our money per year. Set a win/loss ratio and a risk percentage.

2) Get an MT4 broker, get used to the platform and then load in a profile of a dozen or so key charts to act as a guide and reference points each week: our dashboard.

3) Look at the web to gauge what key fundamental events are happening in the forthcoming week.

4) See what the world thinks of that in terms of sentiment.

5) Where the fundamentals and the sentiment are in alignment, identify some potential trades and create a weekly profile of those charts to watch all week.

6) Identify a technical setup from the chart using the candlesticks and indicators loaded.

7) Place the order, set a stop loss and Trade that Chart!

If you want to get access to our weekly trading plan that does all this for you then just click here for details: www.financialinvestingandtrading.com/tradingplan

Key reminders:

1) The strategy is a long term issue – let's say annually.

2) The outline trading plan of fundamentals plus sentiment is weekly.

3) The review of the technicals on the charts and trades is daily.

4) ONLY trade the ONE chart each week that has the best technical set up. The trades will last approximately 7 – 10 days and then you're out. With this regime, at any time you may be in 2 or 3 trades and that's enough for now.

5) If you think a share or an index is going to go up you go LONG – and buy, and if you think the share or index is going to fall then you sell – and go SHORT.

6) With currency, if you think a currency is going to go up, you buy it against another currency in a pair with the best technical set up on the charts, and if you think a currency is weak, you sell it against others.

Always remember that if a chart isn't easily available, you sell the strong currency against another and go short – for instance, if you think the USD is strong you can either BUY and go LONG on the USDJPY or go SHORT and SELL the EURUSD or GBPUSD.

7) Always remember that the JPY is different to all the others and if you think the JPY is strong you SELL it and go short. Conversely if you think the JPY is weak you BUY it.

LET'S TRADE!

Daily Diary

Gill: WOW! I can't believe that we've come so far with this and learned so much, and because it's all process driven and I can follow the steps I'm really confident that we can do this.

Michael: It took a long time to work out that less is more when it comes to looking at charts. When I first started I traded individual stocks via website recommendations and as we know, there are hundreds of stocks in most stock markets so I was looking at charts a lot. This also led me to feeling like I needed to be placing trades all the time and not just when the time is right. Focusing on a few charts based on the fundamentals is what makes trading viable. Also as a recommendation, when starting make sure you keep to reviewing every day even if for only a couple of minutes, after going on my first course I got home and my internet was down for 2 weeks, after this time I got back to it and had no idea what I was doing. Stick with it. And keep a journal of what you do and why.

Week Forty-Three: 19th – 25th February 2018

LESSONS and LEARNINGS: Tier Four

Placing a trade: Part One

When we finally decide to place a trade, we have to decide when to get in and when to get out.

1) When to get **into** a trade is normally a fairly easy decision. We either get in at the market position – i.e. where the price is now on the chart – or we decide to get in after some confirmation of the price direction. For instance, if we think the price is at the bottom of a channel and has hit resistance and we believe the price is going to start moving up, we may set the trade to start when the price HAS started to move up a few PIPs or points, so we have some confirmation that our theory is right before we jump in.

    The first version is called a market trade and the second is called a pending trade.

2) When to get out of a trade is more difficult – especially if we don't want to watch the charts constantly – and in any case, we can't watch a chart 24 hours a day (in the case of a currency trade).

    We set a price at which we want to get out of the trade with a stop loss.

The stop loss

The stop loss has many functions but initially the stop loss is the place we allow the price to go to before we decide the trade has gone wrong!

Let's say we are looking at GBPUSD and we believe the price is going to continue to rise and so we enter the market at the current price of 1.3857.

The data window shows me the close price of the candle I'm looking at. If you remember, the currency market only closes on a Friday at 10.00 and re-opens on the Sunday at 10.00 (so this isn't a real 'close').

Data Window	✕
⟪∿⟫ GBPUSD, Daily	
Date	2018.01.19
Open	1.38916
High	1.39444
Low	1.38381
Close	1.38571
Volume	238033
⟪∿⟫ Indicator window 1	
𝑓ₒ ATR(14)	0.01024

I believe in this instance that the price is going to rise but, just in case it doesn't, I want to set a place to get out, if my belief and my interpretation of the technicals is wrong.

I look at the chart and decide where I'm prepared to allow the price to fall to before I accept that my original belief of a price rise was wrong and I think it will be at about 1.3749 – I've marked that line in bold.

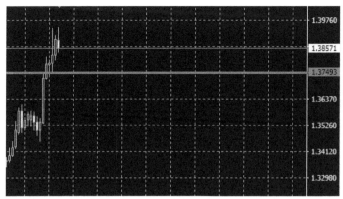

This equates to approximately 108 PIPs (1.3857 – 1.3749) and feels comfortable to me.

I check that stop loss against the ATR which is currently running at 102 PIPs and again, that feels acceptable because if the price moves by the ATR in it's normal volatility then I won't get stopped out (just!) because of that.

I therefore set my trade and my stop loss and place the order.

Then one of two things happen, either:

1) The price drops and I get 'stopped out' and my stop loss has limited the amount I've lost and in accordance with my plan and I feel OK with that, or

2) The price rises.

And in this case, when the price rises sufficiently I then MOVE my stop to my entry price position such that I now know this trade is protected and at worse, I will break even.

N.B. the first rule of trading is to protect your capital and this does that.

Be careful not to bring your stop loss too close however, otherwise you'll be stopped out too quickly and if this trade is going the way we expect we want to let it breath and run, so that our profit is maximised.

As a guide, keep your stop loss at the PIP differential you established at the beginning – in our example case, 108 PIPs.

THEN, as the price continues to rise, keep moving your stop loss up behind the price whilst maintaining the PIP differential – so you allow the trade to 'breathe' naturally, and keep moving it up. This has the effect of protecting your profit.

And from here on you have another choice:

- to just keep doing this until the price turns and you get stopped out and you bank the profit made, or

- you can take profit at where the market is because you think that's the peak (but that involves some predictive guess work or you close part of your deal and leave the remainder to run).

  Experiment with all those options until you find one that works for you. For me, I don't want to watch these charts too often or for too long so I'm content to just let a winning trade be stopped out with my stop loss.

Monitor how you feel emotionally with these stop losses. If you just leave a stop loss to take you out of a winning trade and you bank some profit, do you feel annoyed at the potential profit lost because you didn't come out at EXACTLY the maximum profit position? If so, don't worry about it – you don't go broke leaving some profit on the table and just be content with the profit made and go find the next trade.

Take profit

Some people also set a take profit position when they place an order and they identify exactly where they want to close the deal. However, if the trade is in profit why not let it keep running? But, if you prefer the certainty of knowing exactly how much profit you're going to make – assuming the trade goes in the right direction – then set a take profit.

Trailing stops

It is possible with some automated platforms to set the stop loss as a trailing stop loss and for example we just set the trailing stop at 108 PIPs and the programme will do it for you.

Stop loss tips:

1) Firstly, LOOK at the chart to see where your stop loss should be. If we stick to the ratio of risking 0.5% and planning a 1% gain, the loss should always be half the positive movement we're expecting on the chart.

2) Check that against the ATR – and we would expect a stop loss to be somewhere between about 75% of the daily ATR and about 200%.

3) NEVER move a stop loss into a bigger loss. That is an emotional activity because you're moving the stop

loss so that it won't be hit in a losing trade – after all, the trade is only a loser if it's banked! DON'T do that. If it's a loss then take it quickly and move on.

4) Stop losing trades quickly and let winners run.

Daily Diary

Gill: I can now see that trading is a mixture of technique and emotion. I can also see how easy it would be to move a stop in the 'wrong' direction to be in denial of a loss making trade. But I need to trust the system and place the trades cleanly and in accordance with the formula and just let it work without any fear getting in the way.

Michael: Stop losses are an incredibly helpful tool. Learning where to put them is all part of a learning process. You want them not too far away as to lose more money but not too close as to be stopped out due to general volatility. This is also another reason why we review daily, as your position on your stop will change with the price from day to day. Only ever move a stop up as moving one down means you risk losing more than you were willing to at the start.

Week Forty-Four: 26th February – 4th March 2018

LESSONS and LEARNINGS: Tier Four

Placing a trade: Part Two

a)   Market Order

Taking our previous example of a GBPUSD trade at a market price of 1.3857 and a potential stop loss position of 108 PIPs at a price of 1.3749 I now need to calculate my lot (or order) size. I have the automated risk manager software so I pop those parameters into that.

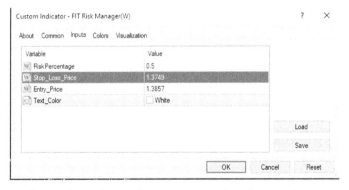

If you don't have the automated software then you need to calculate your lot size.

It tells me that on my (dummy) account of £50,000, and at a risk of 0.5% of my money, then I need to place an order for 0.32 lots.

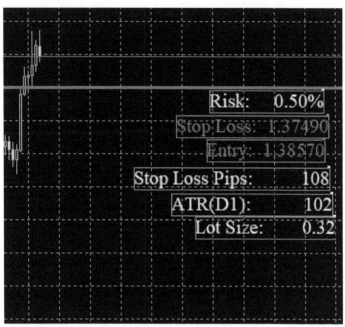

Risk:	**0.50%**
Stop Loss:	**1.37490**
Entry:	**1.38570**
Stop Loss Pips:	**108**
ATR(D1):	**102**
Lot Size:	**0.32**

I can then click on the F9 button and the order sheet comes up.

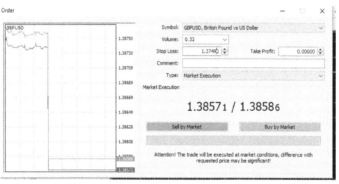

I enter my lot size and my stop loss. I don't want to set a take profit amount or price as I'm going to manage the trade with my stop loss and I then press the buy at Market button.

This will get me into the trade at the current market price of 1.3857 and my order is taken. The order number type and size will then appear on the terminal at the bottom of my account.

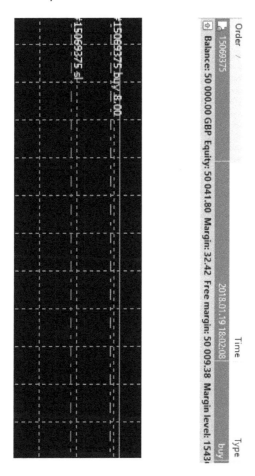

And on the chart, the two orders – the trade and the stop loss – will appear as dotted lines on the chart involved, with the order numbers from the terminal section.

Selling at market

If I wanted to sell at market rather than buy I would do exactly the same. My lots size and risk would be the same but the stop loss would be the other way around.

If my belief was that the price was going to fall rather than rise I would look at the chart differently, but using the same principles. If, for instance, I thought the price was going to fall from 1.3857, I would put my stop loss above the price – because that would be where I knew the trade wasn't going the way I thought, and simplistically, if we use the same 108 PIPs that we've already calculated, my stop loss would be not 1.3479 but 108 PIPs *above* at 1.3965.

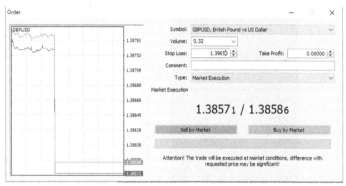

The lot size is still 0.32 but the stop loss line is above the price.

I transpose the figures into the order summary F9 and I press Sell by Market.

b)   Pending Order

Taking exactly the same chart and the same figures I can also set a pending order and if we look at the order box we can click on *Type* and the pending order list will emerge.

This gives me FOUR options on how to trade:

They are:

- Buy Limit which enables you to set a buy order LOWER (ie better) than the current market price – before it rises to where you expect.

- Sell Limit which enables you to set a sell order at a HIGHER (ie better) price – before it falls to where you expect.

- Buy Stop where you set a buy price HIGHER than its current price (i.e. a slightly worse price than now) whilst you wait for confirmation of the price going in the right way.

- Sell Stop where you set a price lower than its current price (i.e. worse than now) while you wait for confirmation that the price is going the right way and dropping.

Of course, these prices may never be reached in the short term and the order not taken, therefore it's wise to set an expiry date on these types of orders otherwise they may be left open for some time and you may have forgotten about it because the order wasn't taken when you had it on your weekly plan but it may be picked up unexpectedly at a later date.

If I click on the expiry button it will give me a drop down calendar and I can choose the expiry date of the potential trade.

Once I've set my type of pending order and my expiry – (if I want one – you can just leave that box blank), you then press PLACE and the order will then be sitting there waiting to fill (or not, if the price isn't reached).

When to use each type of trade

1) Test all types of trade first on a dummy account, so you get familiar with what to place in what box and why.

2) Even with real money, in the first instance I would trade market trades as this gives us the immediate feedback of the order being taken and then we can watch the trade. If the order doesn't do as we expect, or we've placed the order incorrectly, we can close it quickly without much loss or exposure. With a pending order it's very difficult to watch it get taken up and it may be several hours or days before you have the chance to notice any error.

3) With equities and indices there is always an open and close price as the markets close each day. I find that the most predictable prices for equities tend to happen at the end of the day when everybody has finished going in and out and completed their buys and sells, so I like to trade at market with equities and indices an hour or so before closing.

    If I'm operating purely on one country, then I use the closing time for that particular country's exchange and if I'm trading globally, I use the hour or so before New York closes.

4) With currency I will generally do market orders (mainly because it's simpler) but I will consider pending orders if the situation is right.

Report and review

Finally, always make a note of what trades have been

placed and WHY, then watch them play out, add a note to say what happened and whether you can learn anything from the trade, with hindsight.

Record your loss to win ratio and the risk and reward ratios.

Always, trade, record, review and renew the strategy!

Daily Diary

Gill: I still find the order boxes slightly confusing and I have to refer to my notes each time – but that's OK as I know then that I'm safest. I always think it through and write the amounts down before I enter them in the order box just in case the box 'disappears'!

Michael: Buy a diary and write all your trades and why you did them. I'm not joking when I say that I've forgotten why I put on a trade the next day. By recording your trades and reviewing you can work out if your strategy is working and correct, if necessary.

Week Forty-Five: 5th – 11th March 2018

LESSONS and LEARNINGS: Tier Four

Final pieces of the Tier Four puzzle!

There are two final pieces of information we get from the fxpro trading account that we need to look at: the leverage buttons and then finally, the Fibonacci button.

Leverage and the accounting numbers

There is a line at the bottom of the trading screen – the top line in the terminal section – that has lots of numbers. When you first start it will record the amount you have deposited. As you trade it will show other figures and here's one below which has £49,756.97 in three different descriptions.

What this means is that I started with £50k, did a trade and lost £243.03, resulting in £49,756.97 being available still to trade. Because there are no open trades, it shows the same balance as my equity and also my free margin.

> ○ Balance: 49 756.97 GBP Equity: 49 756.97 Free margin: 49 756.97

If we then continue to trade it will then begin to look like this:

> ⊕ Balance: 49 935.68 GBP Equity: 49 913.92 Margin: 175.77 Free margin: 49 738.16 Margin level: 28398.10%

What do each of them mean? In order to understand, we need to start with the concept of leverage.

Leverage

We have set our leverage at 500:1, meaning that we can control 500 times the amount of stock or currency with £/$1. If we had set the leverage at 100:1 we would control or be able to trade 100 times our deposit, so in essence we can trade much larger amounts than we actually have. For example, if our leverage is 100:1 we can buy one basic lot of $100,000 with $1,000.

Balance

This is the amount you started with before all current open trades.

Equity

Is purely your opening balance, as above, and then adjusted for any open positions, with unrealised losses being deducted and unrealised profits added!

Margin or margin required

This is the amount of margin needed to trade each time, and effectively means your exposure. If you go long and buy $1,000 GBPUSD at 1.4095, I have to have $1,409 ($1,000 *1.4095) as required margin to make the trade. This is the collateral that I have to put up to trade. It is my required margin.

When the deal completes the required margin disappears.

Free Margin

Is just the equity figure, less the margin required amount, so the amount left to play with!

Margin Level

Is a percentage figure and is derived by taking the amount of equity divided by the required margin multiplied by 100. This indicates how much 'cover' you have on your open trades.

By monitoring the figures on the accounting line you can immediately see how strong your positions are and how much cover and protection you have in comparison to the amounts exposed on trades. The figures take some getting used to but are worth watching.

Fibonacci Retracement

The Fibonacci retracement tool is on the lower tool bar and has a little F in the bottom right-hand corner.

Fibonacci was a medieval mathematician who discovered what is sometimes called God's blueprint in that he realised that most of nature conforms to a given numerical sequence, which starts with a 0 followed by 1 and then every number is a sum of the previous two. The Fibonacci numbers are therefore 0, 1, 2, 3, 5, 8, 13, 21, and so on and are also nature's numbering system. They appear everywhere in nature, from the leaf arrangement in plants and trees, to the pattern of a bee hive and so on.

Then if we divide one of the numbers by its preceding one we get an outcome known as the golden ratio. If we divide 8 by 5 the number generated is 1.6. As the numbers get larger we get the more accurate Fibonacci ratio of 1.618.

This number is not only prevalent in nature but also in our day to day life. Most of Leonardo da Vinci's canvases are 1 by 1.6, a standard credit card is broadly 1 to 1.6, and it's also the ratio of perfection and if a person's physical measurements are nearer to 1.6 then we are most likely to consider them beautiful.

The length of A divided by 1,62 = The length of B or C
OR
The length of B or C multiplied by 1,62 = The length of A

Look at Her Beautiful Face

To continue the theory, what happens in the trading world is that very commonly share or currency prices follow a Fibonacci sequence, and it is so common that most sophisticated broker systems like fxpro would include a Fibonacci number measure in the tool box.

It is possible to trade off a Fibonacci wave where you monitor a price going up – or down - in 1.6 'steps' and also with fxpro they enable us to measure a Fibonacci retracement, where a price will move and bounce on or off the Fibonacci lines of:

- 61.8% (i.e. the one found by dividing one number in the series by the number that follows it). For example: 8/13 = 0.6153, and 55/89 = 0.6179.

- The 38.2% ratio is found by dividing one number in the series by the number that is found two places to the right. For example: 55/144 = 0.3819.

- The 23.6% ratio is found by dividing one number in the series by the number that is three places to the right. For example: 8/34 = 0.2352.

Then most systems, like fxpro, add a 100% measurement line and a 50% line.

These ratios appear to play an important role in trading, just as they do in nature, and can be used to determine critical points that more often cause a price to reverse.

The direction of the prior trend is likely to continue once the price has fallen back – or retraced – to a Fibonacci point.

If we look at the chart below I have used the Fibonacci tool to draw highlight the top and the bottom of this trend. If we ignore the 50% line (which isn't actually a Fibonacci number and we can delete on the fxpro system if we wish), we can see that the 100% line is at the top of the trend: the 0% is at the bottom and the 61.8% line is almost exactly where the price falls back or retraces to before it continues its upwards journey.

The 38.2% and the 23.6% lines also occur at a point when the price stutters or has a significant bar.

Isn't that amazing!

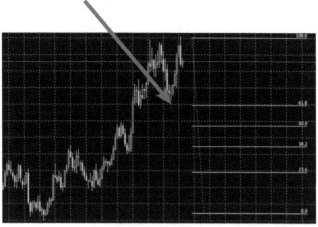

Daily Diary

Gill: I've always been fascinated by Fibonacci and I use it in all my investing and trading and it forms the basis of the strategic Pyramid on both my share activity and my property investing. It's one of those things that doesn't appear to have any logic to it, and I still don't really understand why it works – it just does!

Michael: I've never been overly interested in Fibonacci as it doesn't seem to have a tangible reason for working. However, if you're like me, we still have to look at the Fibonacci because people do believe it affects the market and so it will. This is the effect of sentiment on the market.

Week Forty-Six: 12ᵗʰ – 18ᵗʰ March 2018

LESSONS and LEARNINGS: Tier Four

Tier Four Summary

We have now covered everything we need to be able to trade at Tier Four, so let's look at some example trades.

EURUSD: Channel Break Out

All we ever look at are the charts in our standard dashboard and we're going to look here at the EURUSD, which is one of the two most commonly traded currency pairs.

We've downloaded here the daily EURUSD chart starting from just before our trading year of April 2017 – 2018 begins, and ending with May 2017, partly into our trading year.

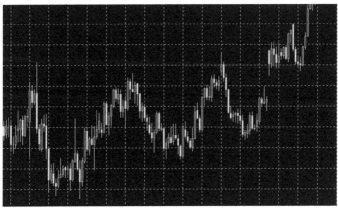

There are several points to note:

1) There appears to be a channel of sorts appearing, with a top and bottom line drawn in below:

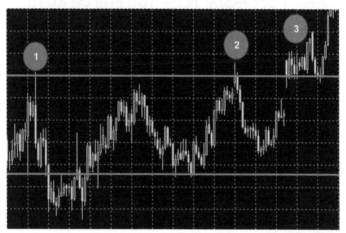

2) The price has had a couple of attempts to break up through the resistance and points 1 and 2 but didn't quite make it. The two bars for the days on the spike points at 1 and 2 are clearly tests; they spike very high during the day but then fall back quickly and close lower. They have very long up wicks:

Here are the relevant candlesticks expanded for illustration:

Point 1:

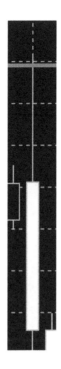

Point 2:

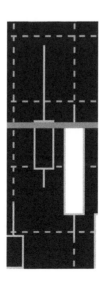

This candlestick is the 27th March 2017, and we can clearly see resistance holding firm at the line we drew earlier, and although the price tries to break through (the up wick) it doesn't hold and the price falls back to resistance by the end of the day.

Then when the break through comes (at point 3) it goes through resistance and once the line is completely breached, the price goes straight up:

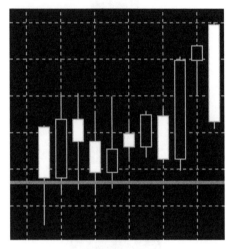

And it continues up for some considerable time, creating a solid upward trend line.

Here is the chart from our starting position to July 2017, and we could have got into the deal at anytime after the resistance was breached and we could have made money on that deal.

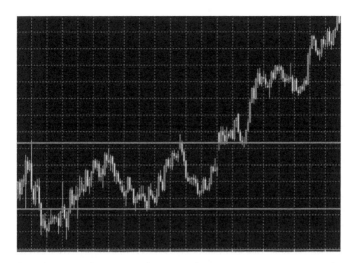

3) There is also a break through support – point 4 on the chart:

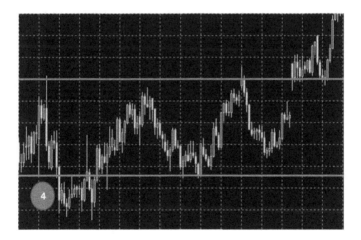

We may have been tempted to put on a sell trade at that point. We may have made money, but it's likely to have been small and as long as we stick to our formula and processes, we should have been stopped out fairly quickly.

And that's OK!

As long as we have more winners than losers (ideally a 60/40 ratio) and the winners are bigger than the losers then we will always make money.

If we look at the chart one last time we can see that the dip below support in the channel is small (bracket and Figure A) and yet the break through resistance is large (bracket and Figure B). In fact, the rise in B is almost four times the fall in A – that's a great win to loss ratio.

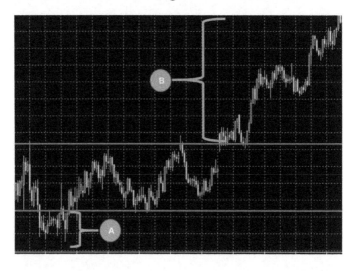

US Stock Indices: Trend reversal

We started our trading test year in April 2017, at a time when the US stock market was riding high and on a severe upward trend.

I've included the NASDAQ, and the S&P 500 to show the same trend reflected in two different charts; the time scale starts when we did, in April 2017 and goes to the end of January 2018:

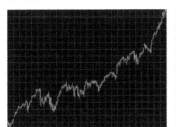 

The trend lines are almost identical.

And then the trend reversed – massively. If we go back to our basic premise of

F undamental +

S entiment +

T echnical

We can see that in January 2018 the US market sentiment felt that the rise had taken stocks too far; there was a fundamental change in how the US economy was viewed.

There was an announcement of wage increases and a fear that inflation was rising too fast, and as we know from our knowledge of fundamentals, that generally means that interest rates will rise.

When interest rates rise, the 'sentiment' in the market place moves to going out of stocks and into bonds.

In summary, the fundamentals suggested a market correction, the sentiment suggested investors leaving the stock market and the technicals showed an all time high, followed by the trend reversing and the market falling:

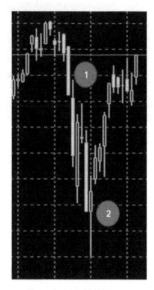
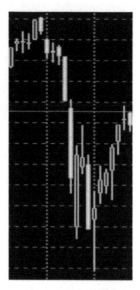

Again, the trends are almost identical with both the NASAQ and the S&P showing their lowest figures on the 9th February 2018.

Knowing about the fundamentals and the sentiment we could have got into the trade as soon as the trend started to reverse (at about point 1) and traded this all the way down (with a sell order), with a stop loss protecting the profit as it fell. I suspect we would have been stopped out on the 9th February at point 2 as again we have a very long wick on the candlestick, indicating that prices have tested lower but not stuck. That's an indicator of the next reversal back up.

The trade down was from approximately 6,800 to 6,300 – that's a massive 500 points. We only needed to have been in part of that movement to have made a significant sum. We can never exactly identify the start of a trend reversal and the stopping of it at the end – but as long as we're in most of it that's good enough to make profits.

Summary

We've now gone completely through everything we need to know in order to trade at Tier Four. At this level it's less important *what* is traded and more important that we understand the *why* of the trade. The why comes down to the broad fundamentals – of the national or global economy, together with some idea of how the world views that generally: this is the sentiment, and then we look for technical set ups within a chart that endorse the fundamentals and sentiment to find a deal to trade. At this stage the technical we're looking specifically for are:

- Channels – and bounces off the channels
- Break outs through the support and resistance lines of the channel
- Trend lines and reversals – off new highs and new lows.

There is much more to learn, of course: for instance, the long wick on a candlestick that we have briefly covered here is an indicator of another strategy to learn; there are also many chart formations to trade from other than just a channel, such as a head and shoulders formation, double tops (and bottoms, of course), and inverse formations. These are all for advanced learning.

For now, we can paper trade and watch trading activity at Tier Four until we are comfortable enough to trade real money.

Going forward

As an organisation we monitor the fundamentals and the sentiment. We publish weekly trading plans, daily trades and have a daily alert video, as well as reviews and monitoring. We even hold a regular weekly Q & A webinar. If you're interested in joining us on that then please contact us on:

www.financialinvestingandtrading.com or call 01803 866986

Daily Diary

Gill: I realised in writing my part of this chapter that I have learned an awful lot since we started. I know enough to identify a trade and the reasons why a potential trade appears on a chart. I'm also totally content with the concept of losing sometimes, and as long as I keep the win/loss ratios correct, then I will always win overall. It's a huge relief to realise that I don't have to win or make profit on every single trade – I'm not that perfect!

Michael: This is all too much at the start but just looking at charts and researching the F,S,T, you do start to get it, trust me! Now when I see charts I see potential trades or not as the case may be.

7. Tier Five

Week Forty-Seven: 19th – 25th March 2018

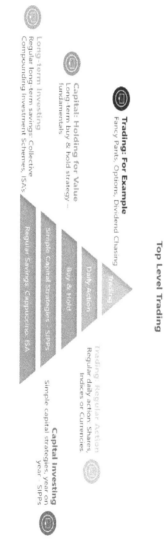

LESSONS and LEARNINGS

TIER FIVE: Overview

Top Level Trading

Trading: For Example
Fancy Pants, Options, Dividend Chasing

Capital: Holding for Value
Long-term buy & hold strategy –
fundamentals

Long-term Investing
Regular long-term savings. Collective
Compounding Investment Schemes, ISAs

Trading Regular Action
Regular daily action. Shares,
Indices or Currencies

Capital Investing
Simple capital strategies, year on
year - SIPPs

Regular Savings Cappuccino. ISA
Simple Capital Strategies - SIPPs
Buy & Hold
Daily Action
Trading

We are now at the very top of the Pyramid and at this level of trading – anything goes!

At this stage anything you might want to trade (oil, diamonds, gold) and however you want to do it is a potential strategy. At this stage you can trade for income or capital or potentially, both.

Here's some ideas on what to invest or trade with:

1) Penny stocks. This involves finding very cheap stocks (hence the penny) and watching them grow into pounds! What you're looking for here is the 'next best thing' and this is a very speculative long term capital strategy, and involves some detailed research on the individual companies concerned.

2) Dividend chasing is a purely income strategy based on dividend distribution dates. The idea is to get the right to receive the dividend just the day before that entitlement stops (the ex-dividend date), get the entitlement to the dividend, then sell immediately and then receive the dividend itself. This idea works well in theory but so often the price of a stock reflects the expected dividend anyway, so very little is gained: you gain the income but when you sell the share the price has dropped by an equivalent amount. Choose carefully with this one.

3) Stock splits is another capital strategy and the plan with this one is to buy a share or stock that is about to – or is likely to be – split at some stage in the future. Let's say a share in ABC plc is worth £4 and is about to split. The intention of the company doing

the splitting is partly to make their shares more affordable and let's say they do a 2 for 1 split and every person with a share gets one additional 'free' share. But as a result of that, unless there's any other change in the company fundamentals, the price will drop from £4 to £2.

However, over time a share will often revert or drift back to its original price of £4, and a significant capital gain is made.

4) Trading very frequently: day trading. This is more of an income strategy because the money is gained (or lost) very quickly.

5) Arbitrage: Arbitrage is the simultaneous purchase and sale of a stock or index or currency to profit from the differences in price that occur when the asset is traded on different markets or in different forms. The profit arises due to those differences and the inefficiency of the markets to reconcile the two different forms immediately. However, those inefficiencies get smaller all the time due to global consolidation and computer speeds, and this is a very time intensive strategy.

6) Derivatives: these don't really merit a section of their own as they are purely trading products that are derived from one, or a combination of, others.

7) Warrants: a warrant is an example of a derivative and is like an option as it gives the owner the right but not the obligation to buy a share at a given price at a given date in the future. It differs from an option in that a warrant is issued by an individual company and is not

a 'free market' asset traded everywhere. Commonly, warrants are issued by a company as part of a new share offering as a 'bonus'. Like options, you can get a call warrant or a put warrant. This is a very specific strategy and would need a lot of research into the company concerned.

8) Hedging: A hedge is just an investment position intended to offset mainly, potential losses and act as a type of insurance against a big negative position. A hedge can be constructed – or derived - from many types of financial instruments, including shares, options and futures.

Other than those – and there would be many others that we could list here – there are only three that we will cover here: Options, Commodities and Futures

9) Options: like a warrant, an option gives the holder either the right or the obligation to trade an asset at some time in the future and a given price. They are freely traded and exist in many different forms, timescales and price points. We will cover options shortly.

10) Commodities: like oil and wheat and we will include a section purely on that later.

11) Futures contracts are purely that: a contract to buy or sell something in the future and we will briefly mention those as part of the commodities section.

Tier Five Tips:

1) LEARN as much as you can about it and don't do anything unless you're certain that you know what you're doing!

2) Separate out a section of your time and your money (when you get to real money), that's you can evaluate this portion of your trading in isolation. If you know how much time you're spending, you can assess the level of return you need to make. Compare the time versus reward from this activity to other activities at all the other Tiers, and compare to other activities you're doing at Tier Five.

3) TEST, test and test again: test the strategy, test the system, test the process and test the trades – all in theory or on paper before you release any money.

4) As you test, constantly review and tweak your plan until you have accuracy.

5) When you start trading with real money make sure those funds are isolated and segregated in order to get an accurate report on returns. Ideally, start a new broker account.

6) Set and test a clear strategy, keep a trading diary so you know WHY you did something: record your analysis and thought processes.

7) Set a clear stop loss or protection strategy.

THEN do it a little bit, check the results and then review your whole investment and trading strategies again to identify where this new trading fits. It could be that as a result of this new trading, you flex your whole Pyramid of investments and change your strategies.

DAILY DIARY

Gill: I have to be honest and say that Tier Five leaves me feeling a bit out of my depth. But like anything I know that the more I learn the less I will feel like that and any detailed learning or knowledge removes fear. However, I currently don't intend to be very active at Tier Five and I will probably concentrate my learning on just trading options.

Michael: A lot of traders I know, when it comes to top tier trading, focus on one aspect, whether it's something they are interested in or they worked in before e.g. working with pharmaceuticals. So a useful start for you getting to this stage may be getting very familiar with a certain industry or currency so you can move into options or futures within a particular field.

Week Forty-Eight: 26ᵗʰ March – 1ˢᵗ April 2018

Tier Five: Options

Options are a basic strategy at Tier Five and the only one we will cover here in any detail but please get appropriate training and support if you want to trade options as this is a technical and risky area, so please stay safe.

Definitions

Option

An option is an agreement between two parties to buy or sell an asset.

The buyer has the right to buy an asset (such as a stock, commodity, or currency) at a certain price at a certain time in the future, and the option buyer pays an options premium for that right.

The buyer has the *right* but not the obligation to buy, and if the buyer changes their mind and doesn't buy – or take up the option – then that's fine and all they have lost is their option premium. The buyer can decide at any time from the time they buy the option to the expiry time, whether to take it up or not.

The same can work for buying an option to sell and in that case you buy an option to sell at a given time.

When you buy an option to buy, that's called a call option and when you buy an option to sell, that's called a put option.

You would buy a call option if you think the price is going to rise (so you have the right to get the shares cheaper) and you buy a put option if you think it's going down (so you have the right to sell them at a higher price).

This is the simplest and less risky way to trade options – and it can act as insurance or cover – or hedge - for other activity.

Expiry and exercise
The option expires at the given time and it needs to be exercised before the expiry time or it just expires!

The Premium
The premium is the price you pay for the option: these are published by the markets who buy and sell options and you can look them up before you buy like you can with any other trading instrument.

Strike Price
The strike price is the price agreed for the transaction of the asset when the time comes.

Selling options
Selling – called writing - options works just as for buying options but the other way around! However, the risk can be perceived as much larger because you are selling an obligation (i.e. you have to do it), whereas when you buy options you are buying the right to but not the obligation

to, so you have the choice whether to take it or not. When you sell options, you have no choice.

European and American options
European options can only be traded or bought and sold only at the end whereas US options can trade at any time – so it's better to trade US options.

Chicago Options Exchange
The Chicago Options Exchange is the centre for all options trading. Have a look on www.cboe.com

Long or short
There are four scenarios here, dependent on whether you are the buyer or the seller and whether you buy/sell a put or a call:

If you buy a call – you're long
If you sell (write) a put option – you're also long
If you buy a put option – you're short
If you sell (write) a call option – you're also short

For our purposes, we should really only be a buyer at this early stage as we want to have the right but not any obligations, therefore our positions will be:

Buy an option to buy in the future – LONG
Buy an option to sell in the future – SHORT

And that's more or less how we record long and short on our other Tier Four trading.

A long call option

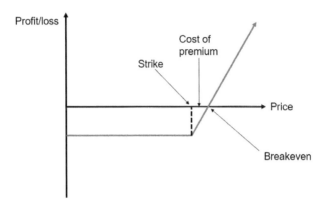

A long put option

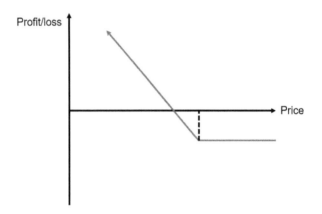

Wasting assets

Options are different to anything else we trade because it has no intrinsic value in or of itself, and the closer to the expiry time then the less the option is worth: hence it is known as a wasting asset.

Options have no value at the expiry time other than if

they are 'in the money'.

In or out the money

Being in the money means that your trade has worked and you've made some profit at the expiry time. For instance, you saw a share priced at $2 and you thought it was likely to rise to $3 in three months, you could buy a call option to buy that share at $2.50 in three months' time. The share price does rise as you expected, and you then take up your right and buy the stock at $2.50, so you are in the money by $0.50 per share!

Out the money is clearly the reverse, and if you did the same trade but the share price fell to $1.50 you are then out the money and you would just let the option expire, and not take up your right to buy.

At the money means that the strike price is more or less the same as the current, tradable price of the asset concerned.

Options Premium Pricing: Time Value

An option's premium is calculated from the sum of combination of its intrinsic value and its time value. We know broadly that an option has no intrinsic value so that equates to the amount it's 'in the money' at any time.

Time value represents the possibility of the option increasing in value, so the more likely an event is to occur then the higher the time value and the more expensive the option will be: this time value is also known as the extrinsic value.

Daily Diary

Gill: As I've gone through this step by step it has all made sense! Pulling it all together into a real trade may be more difficult but if we take it one small step at a time, we can get there.

Michael: Options are something I've struggled with for a while now. I'm not much of a risk taker so I've never used my own money in an options trade (thank you, demo accounts). My main problem is that I don't spend enough time researching to be confident of an outcome. However, if you are really savvy and keen, the rewards are massive.

Week Forty-Nine: 2nd – 8th April 2018

Tier Five: Options
OPTIONS: Detail
A Long Call option

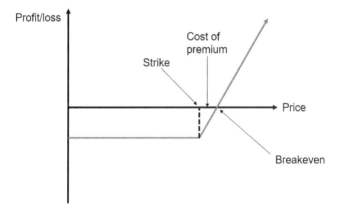

Here we are buying an option to buy something at the given time. Some people would consider the breakeven point to be when the share price reaches the strike price of the option, but it's safer to include the premium cost as well, as that is a cost to this particular trade. Hence, the breakeven position is higher along the price line. As soon as the share price goes above the strike price this trade is 'in the money'.

EXAMPLE OF A LONG CALL

Let's say Microsoft (MSFT) is trading at $40, and we wanted to buy 1,000 shares. That would cost us $40,000. But with an option we can still control that amount of shares for much less cost, and purchase a call option (to buy in the future) and let's say it is now August and there is a call option in one month at a strike price of $40 for $1 per contract.

The contract details and the price would say:

Buy 10 MSFT SEP 40 Call at $1.00 i.e. buy 10 Microsoft contracts (of 100 shares each = 1,000 shares controlled). The share option being bought is Microsoft (MSFT); the expiry date is September, the strike price is $40 and it's a call (buy) option.

You would buy a call option if you think the price is going to rise.

Even though the trade is in contracts we pay the $1 *per share*. Therefore, the cost to us is $1,000, being $1 times 100 shares.

We can then control 1,000 Microsoft shares for $1,000 rather than the $40,000 we would need to buy them outright.

If the price of the shares then rises to say, $45 we make $5 per share i.e. $5,000. If it doesn't, we've lost our $1,000 but the trading ratio is different there: we are risking only $1,000 for the opportunity of a much larger gain.

N.B. expiry dates are uniform and tend to be the third Friday in each month.

Short Put option

If we thought the price was going to fall we might buy a (short) put option to sell the shares, and in that case the information would be:

Buy 10 MSGT SEP 40 Put at $1.00

If you bought this option, you would have the right to sell at $40: if you think the price is going to fall to say, $30 you would then have a 'guaranteed' buyer at $40 and you make $10 per share.

You buy a put if you think the price is going down.

Price charts

If we look at an options pricing table for MSFT we can see the options expiry dates available to us for March 2018: they are each Friday in March so we can trade weekly, two weekly, three weekly, four weekly or monthly options.

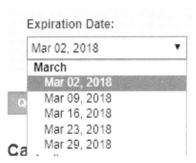

Then, once we've selected our expiry date we click again on the pricing table to see the prices and options availlable:

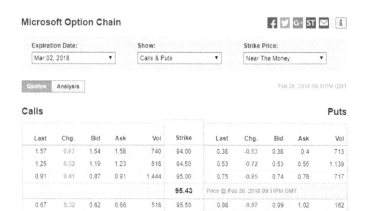

Microsoft Option Chain

Expiration Date: Mar 02, 2018 ▼ | Show: Calls & Puts ▼ | Strike Price: Near The Money ▼

Quotes | Analysis — Feb 26, 2018 09:11PM GMT

Calls / Puts

Last	Chg.	Bid	Ask	Vol	Strike	Last	Chg.	Bid	Ask	Vol
1.57	0.67	1.54	1.58	740	94.00	0.38	-0.53	0.38	0.4	713
1.25	0.52	1.19	1.23	618	94.50	0.53	-0.72	0.53	0.55	1.139
0.91	0.41	0.87	0.91	1.444	95.00	0.75	-0.85	0.74	0.76	717
					95.43 Price @ Feb 26, 2018 09:11PM GMT					
0.67	0.32	0.62	0.66	518	95.50	0.98	-0.97	0.99	1.02	162
0.45	0.2	0.45	0.47	2.593	96.00	1.36	-1.79	1.28	1.31	165
0.32	0.17	0.3	0.32	1.359	96.50	1.75	-1.03	1.65	1.68	9

The table provides us with the cost per contract 1.57 for example on the top line and the $95.43 in the centre of the table shows us the current price so we can see if we're on the money, out or at the money.

If we can buy a call for less than the share price we're in the money; if we can sell a put for more than the current price we're in the money on that side.

The columns show us:

Last: the price that particular option was last traded at.

Chg (Change) : Change is how much the Last price has changed since the previous close.

Bid: The price at which buyers are trying to buy the option and the price at which you sell.

Ask: The price at which sellers are trying to sell the option and the price at which you buy.

Vol (Volume): Tells you how many contracts have been traded during the session.

N.B. Options that have large volume typically have a

tighter Bid-Ask spread since more traders are looking to get in and out of positions.

You can also normally see the:

Open Int (Interest) which is the number of open positions in that contract.

Naked calls

This is such an odd term in options trading I just thought I'd mention it! All it means is that you're selling calls on stuff you don't own. Selling or writing calls is not for the faint-hearted and I would stick with just *buying* calls or puts in the early days.

The Greek Stuff

You don't get far in any learning about options before you get confronted by the Greeks because the Greek letters denote a calculation that helps you evaluate various options positions. The most common of these are:

Delta: which measures the options price sensitivity in relation to the underlying asset. It is expressed in the range of 0 to 1 for call options and 0 to -1, and the nearer to 1 or -1 the Delta the more valuable the option.

Gamma: measures how much the options Delta changes when the price of the underlying asset changes. The range is again, 1 to -1.

Rho: measures how much the premium for an option changes with interest rates. In theory, if interest rates go up then the premium on calls will rise and the premium for puts will fall.

Theta: measures the sensitivity of the option to the time wastage, calculating how much the option will lose for each day nearer the exiry date.

All options trading platforms will show the value of the Greeks for every contract on their system.

Here's an example showing March figures for IBM:

OpSym	Bid (pts)	Ask (pts)	Extrinsic Bid/Ask (pts)	IV Bid/Ask (%)	Delta Bid/Ask (%)	Gamma Bid/Ask (%)	Vega Bid/Ask (pts/%p IV)	Theta Bid/Ask (pts/day)	Volume	Open Interest	Strike
IBM MAR10 110 C	16.25	16.70	0.00 / 0.37	19.77 / 35.15	99.16 / 92.06	0.27 / 1.15	0.007 / 0.053	-0.0009 / -0.0279	0	479	110.000
IBM MAR10 115 C	11.65	11.80	0.32 / 0.47	25.37 / 27.68	90.52 / 88.67	1.82 / 1.90	0.060 / 0.069	-0.0227 / -0.0290	47	552	115.000
IBM MAR10 120 C	7.15	7.30	0.82 / 0.97	21.85 / 23.30	79.89 / 78.51	3.53 / 3.45	0.101 / 0.105	-0.0344 / -0.0385	360	1179	120.000
IBM MAR10 125 C	3.40	3.50	2.07 / 2.17	19.04 / 19.75	58.20 / 57.98	5.65 / 5.46	0.141 / 0.141	-0.0431 / -0.0448	1269	5782	125.000
Stock											126.33
IBM MAR10 130 C	1.10	1.14	1.10 / 1.14	17.41 / 17.73	28.66 / 29.04	5.40 / 5.33	0.123 / 0.124	-0.0349 / -0.0358	1868	5947	130.000
IBM MAR10 135 C	0.23	0.25	0.23 / 0.25	16.73 / 17.08	8.45 / 8.91	2.56 / 2.61	0.056 / 0.058	-0.0154 / -0.0164	666	6539	135.000
IBM MAR10 140 C	0.04	0.06	0.04 / 0.06	17.04 / 18.12	1.82 / 2.47	0.72 / 0.80	0.016 / 0.021	-0.0045 / -0.0062	80	4284	140.000
IBM MAR10 145 C	0.00	0.02	0.00 / 0.03	0.00 / 21.03	0.00 / 1.17	0.00 / 0.40	0.000 / 0.011	-0.0000 / -0.0038	10	1747	145.000

Summary

Trading at Tier Five is risky and all we've been able to do in two sessions with options for instance, is to scratch the surface and understand the basic definitions. If you really want to trade here – and it can be very lucrative – then please seek further education!

Daily Diary

Gill: WOW! Options are complicated, and there is so much to learn. I have no doubt that done properly this is a very high profit activity but I feel the need to read another 10 books on the subject first. This learning hasn't come naturally to me.

Michael: Options are an avenue for the future for me and aren't something I would be comfortable investing in from only reading one book. I hope we have shown their potential. For those of you that find everything else easy there is more to get your teeth into once you've finished this book.

Week Fifty: 9th – 15th April 2018

Tier Five: Commodities and Futures

After options, probably the next most common trading at Tier Five is commodities trading, which in the main is transacted through a futures contract. There is no way anyone should consider this without a lot of knowledge, plus a lot of support, and supported training!

What's a commodity?

Commodities dealing or trading is an age old profession – far older than dealing in stocks, shares, currency or bonds. Ancient civilizations traded a wide range of commodities. It was in search of some commodities, such as spices, that the original explorers started their quest across the globe. Even in those early days commodity dealers would fund explorers or trade on the possibility of a good harvest, crop or trip to the Indies with the aim of making some money on the outcome.

As time progressed, traders used commodities trading as a way to diversify a portfolio, particularly as commodities commonly move in the opposite direction to stocks.

Nowadays, it's fairly easy for a non-professional to

trade a commodity, via a commodities exchange. The main market in the world is the Chicago Mercantile Exchange. The commodities futures market is a standard trading market and is 'open' from Sunday p.m. to Friday p.m.

Types of Commodities

There is a very long list of potential commodities to trade and certainly at least 50, but in the main there are only a dozen or so that people would be familiar with and commonly trade. They are divided into four categories falling into two groups of commodities: hard and soft.

Broadly, hard commodities are 'mined' and soft commodities are 'grown'.

Hard Commodities include:

Metals: gold, silver platinum and copper.
Energy: crude oil, heating oils, natural gas and other gasolines.

Soft Commodities include:

Livestock and meats: hogs, pork bellies, live cattle and feeder cattle.
Agricultural: corn, soya bean, wheat, rice, cocoa, coffee, cotton and sugar.

How to invest in commodities

The most common way to invest in a commodity is through a futures contract, where you agree to buy or sell a specific quantity of a commodity at some given date in the future, at a given price. Futures prices are publicly quoted and futures contracts are available to trade on most types of commodity.

Commodity futures contracts were originally designed to allow farmers to hedge – or insure – against changes in the prices of their crops between planting and when they could be harvested and brought to market. Buying the futures contract cost them money but it protected them against complete financial disaster if their crop failed.

But, in the main, the physical commodity is not traded and the financial trading of the 'paper' commodity far outnumbers the number of transactions where anything is physically bought or delivered. It is estimated that only 2% of all commodities contracts are actually for physical delivery.

The risks are different with commodities compared to say an index or a stock because the price of commodities can be driven by factors that tend to be unpredictable, such as the weather, which can completely ruin or create an abundant crop (and the weather appears to becoming increasingly unpredictable) or epidemics in diseases that affect livestock, or other natural or man-made disasters. Consequently, prices are volatile and trading is incredibly risky. No one should ever allocate a significant proportion of their pot of money to commodities trading.

Some Trading Specifics

Commodity futures are traded in contracts and for example, with crude oil, one contract equates to 1,000 barrels of oil. Each futures contract of corn, on the other hand, represents 5,000 bushels – or about 127 metric tons of corn. Each contract is different and represents a different quantity of the commodity being traded. In the main, this doesn't matter because it's purely one contract of anything to trade but of course, it makes a big difference on the trading price of the contract concerned. Almost all futures are bought and sold on margin, where the total contract is held or controlled by only a small fraction of the real price of the commodity involved. Therefore, the leverage is substantial and there is a risk to losing far more money than you actually place on the trade.

You can trade some futures on a standard broking account like the fxpro trading account we already have but in some cases you may need open another broker account such as Options Express, that will allow you to trade some of the contracts.

The criteria are the same as any other trading at Tiers Four and Five; you need the fundamentals, some concept of sentiment and then the technical positions, and these are broadly the same for commodity futures as they are for our normal Tier Four trading. The technicals specifically are the same and we get charts and candlesticks in the same way and as we recognise.

In addition, we can trade the same technical strategies of watching channels, looking for break outs, monitoring trends, and bounces.

A stop loss is also more or less the same and what you do there is to buy an opposite contract before the future date is reached to match it out and the contract is then offset.

Non-Commodity Futures

Of course it is also possible to trade different – or non-commodity – futures in other instruments that are more familiar to us from other trading at Tier Four, indices such as the S&P 500, currencies or even specific stocks.

Whereas futures can be traded with many different types of asset; commodities tend to only be traded as futures contracts.

Daily Diary

Gill: In the *Toy Story* films there's a pink pig called Hamm and in one of the films he falls down a lift shaft and as he falls another character says: "I can see Pork Bellies are going down". Not often you get a commodities joke in a children's film!

Michael: It's fun trading commodities because the things you are buying feel more real. I only really ever trade oil and gold, like most traders, but it still makes me feel like a tycoon.

Week Fifty-One: 16th – 22nd April 2018

Conclusions

We are fast approaching the end of this year-long experiment and we have learned and studied and listened and read and attended courses and the year has flown by.

We started with a blank page and a few concepts, an overall aim to achieve a 10% return on our money, and 'hope in our hearts' but not much else.

During the year we have achieved our financial aim – or at least we're well on the way to – but what has been a bonus is all the other things we've learned that we can take forward into our financial future.

1) On a strategic level we've discovered that the Pyramid structure that we've used elsewhere on our property investments works just as well for shares! What the Pyramid does is to give a framework of balance and growth, ensuring that time and risk are managed appropriately. It proves that the increasing return as you go up the Pyramid into the different Tiers increases the return almost exactly as it does for property investing.

   And the Pyramid picture says an awful lot more than thousands of words. Everyone gets it!

Top Level Trading

Trading: For Example
Fancy Pants, Options, Dividend Chasing

Capital: Holding for Value
Long-term buy & hold strategy – fundamentals

Long-term Investing
Regular long-term savings, Collective Compounding Investment Schemes, ISA's

Trading

Daily Action

Buy & Hold

Simple Capital Strategies - SIPPs

Regular Savings: Cappuccino ISA

Trading: Regular Action
Regular daily action: Shares, Indices or Currencies

Capital Investing
Simple capital strategies, year on year – SIPPs

2) In Tier One we know how to embrace and invest regular savings into the stock market overall by investing small amounts over the long term into funds that track or mirror the standard market indices in whatever country we like!

This provides long term stability to the overall portfolio and can just trundle along over time and as time flies then the fund increases. We also know that it increases a whole lot more if the funds accumulate the dividends, rather than pay them out as income.

Every man, woman and child should do Tier One as a matter of course – we all need to set up that small regular monthly payment as soon as we can – and even better if our parents do that for us when were born – and just let that darn thing roll and accumulate over time. It becomes almost subliminal, forget about it and just allow it to surprise you one day with how big it's grown.

3) In Tier Two we now know how to take that simple principle up a notch and invest in a few select shares from any of the main indices, choosing the ones most likely to grow more than the average over time.

This is incredibly easy to do and needs very little maintenance apart from an annual review and potential change.

This is slightly more sophisticated as a strategy that the blanket cover created in Tier One but it does tend to outperform that overall fund approach by a percentage or two but it does require a little bit of capital: maybe $/£3k.

4) In Tier Three we discovered that we need to pay attention to individual company facts, figures and accounts with the aim of picking the shares in the companies with the biggest potential. This strategy was hard but with a little bit of attention and sticking to a newly found formula of 8 key things to research, we know we can get a decent return over time.

   In Tier Three it was much easier to invest for dividends and income, and at this level we created choice in our returns.

5) We spent a lot of time learning about Tier Four and the concepts of trading for the first time. There was much to learn but we have condensed that down into three areas: fundamentals, sentiment and then the technical signs generated on charts.

   At this level we discovered that it didn't really matter WHAT you traded (shares, currency, indices, oil, or gold) because it was more about HOW to trade, rather than the asset itself.

   This was definitely a short term strategy, requiring time and attention each day.

6) We never got very far on Tier Five other than to establish what it might look like: commodities, options, warrants and any 'odd' strategy clearly fits in here. However, we quickly realised that any trading at this level needed an awful lot more work and time than we had in this particular experiment – perhaps that's one for next year!

   But it is certainly not for the faint-hearted.

7) Overall, we realised that returns get higher the

more time and effort you make! Tiers One and Two especially were very easy to learn and cover and very quick to implement – those Tiers really require very little input at all, so we were able to cover them in a few short sessions.

Tier Three took a few sessions on its own as it needed more background learning, and Tier Four took the longest time – and the biggest chunk of our year - as it required a lot of research to get going but, as a consequence, the returns are higher.

In summary

This has been easy! But different to what we planned. For instance, we aimed to spend an equal amount of time on each Tier but clearly that wasn't necessary. The bottom Tiers are simple and quick and the top Tiers aren't!

Although we fully intended to trade at Tier Five by the end of the year we soon realised that was never going to be possible: not all Tiers of the Pyramid are equal.

And the overall lesson we learned from the year is that this IS POSSIBLE for anyone: mum and son, friends and family, individual or group. We CAN all do it and we CAN all make a difference – how great is that?

Daily Diary

Gill: Well what an achievement and it's one of those weird experiences that you don't know how far you've come until you look back and remember where you started. Each step has been relatively painless and in retrospect, all the challenges we faced at the time have just disappeared and been forgotten. The saying is true – if you keep your face to the sun, you don't notice the clouds!

Michael: I'm really happy I got this sorted and at an early age. Not just because it means more money in the future but also it is nice to get it out of the way. With my generation, I know a lot of my peers know they won't be able to rely entirely on their allotted pensions, so it's a big weight off my shoulders.

Week Fifty-Two: 23rd – 30th April 2018

THE END!

I'm sitting writing this early in the morning on Tuesday 1st May 2018, and our year's experiment is officially UP!

I downloaded the portfolio yesterday and the two portions look like this below: the UK portion is up 1.11% and the US portion is up 6.99%.

And I'm delighted with that – so far!

30th April

Symbol	Links	Qty	Description	Price	Price Change $	Price Change %	Market Value	Book Cost	Gain / Loss $	Gain / Loss %
:VX	Buy Sell 🔗 ↗ ℹ	115	CHEVRON CORPORATION COM USD0.75	$131.75	-$0.60	-0.45%	$15,151.25	$12,514.03	$2,637.22	21.07%
SCO	Buy Sell 🔗 ↗ ℹ	390	CISCO SYSTEMS INC COM USD0.001	$41.21	$0.02	0.05%	$16,071.90	$12,468.28	$3,603.62	28.90%
O	Buy Sell 🔗 ↗ ℹ	265	COCA-COLA CO COM USD0.25	$46.80	-$0.01	-0.02%	$12,402.00	$12,144.50	$257.50	2.12%
OM	Buy Sell 🔗 ↗ ℹ	160	EXXON MOBIL CORPORATION COM NPV	$87.75	-$0.24	-0.28%	$14,040.00	$12,498.98	$1,541.02	12.33%
E	Buy Sell 🔗 ↗ ℹ	495	GENERAL ELECTRIC CO COM USD0.06	$17.06	-$0.29	-1.65%	$8,444.70	$12,491.68	$-4,046.98	-32.40%
NTC	Buy Sell 🔗 ↗ ℹ	345	INTEL CORP COM USD0.001	$44.38	-$0.01	-0.02%	$15,311.10	$12,531.28	$2,779.82	22.18%
BM	Buy Sell 🔗 ↗ ℹ	90	INTERNATIONAL BUS MACH CORP COM USD0.20	$169.28	$0.63	0.37%	$15,235.20	$12,837.28	$2,397.92	18.68%
RK	Buy Sell 🔗 ↗ ℹ	200	MERCK & CO INC COM USD0.50	$61.09	-$0.94	-1.52%	$12,218.00	$12,541.78	$-323.78	-2.58%
FE	Buy Sell 🔗 ↗ ℹ	375	PFIZER INC COM USD0.05	$36.90	-$0.27	-0.73%	$13,837.50	$12,510.28	$1,327.22	10.61%
Z	Buy Sell 🔗 ↗ ℹ	255	VERIZON COMMUNICATIONS COM USD0.10	$52.74	$1.03	1.99%	$13,448.70	$12,393.13	$1,055.57	8.52%
							$136,160.35	$124,931.22	$11,229.13	8.99%

www.financialinvestingandtrading.com

US Markets prices delayed by 15 min or more

Edit columns   Refresh Prices

Print 🖨   Export 🗎   🔍 Search

Symbol	Links	Qty	Description	Price	Price Change $	Price Change %	Market Value	Book Cost	Gain / Loss $	Gain / Loss %
CVX	Buy Sell	115	CHEVRON CORPORATION COM USD0.75	$127.45	$0.85	0.67%	$14,656.75	$12,514.03	$2,142.72	17.12%
CSCO	Buy Sell	390	CISCO SYSTEMS INC COM USD0.001	$45.01	$0.31	0.68%	$17,553.90	$12,468.28	$5,085.62	40.79%
KO	Buy Sell	265	COCA-COLA CO COM USD0.25	$43.59	$0.29	0.67%	$11,551.35	$12,144.50	$-593.15	-4.88%
XOM	Buy Sell	160	EXXON MOBIL CORPORATION COM NPV	$78.20	$0.41	0.53%	$12,512.00	$12,498.98	$13.02	0.10%
GE	Buy Sell	495	GENERAL ELECTRIC CO COM USD0.06	$14.27	$-0.10	-0.73%	$7,063.65	$12,491.68	$-5,428.03	-43.45%
INTC	Buy Sell	345	INTEL CORP COM USD0.001	$52.99	$0.27	0.51%	$18,281.55	$12,531.28	$5,750.27	45.89%
IBM	Buy Sell	90	INTERNATIONAL BUS MACH CORP COM USD0.20	$146.71	$0.23	0.16%	$13,203.90	$12,837.28	$366.62	2.86%
MRK	Buy Sell	200	MERCK & CO INC COM USD0.50	$59.85	$0.39	0.65%	$11,970.00	$12,541.78	$-571.78	-4.56%
PFE	Buy Sell	375	PFIZER INC COM USD0.05	$37.11	$0.12	0.32%	$13,916.25	$12,510.28	$1,405.97	11.24%
VZ	Buy Sell	255	VERIZON COMMUNICATIONS COM USD0.10	$50.82	$-0.74	-1.44%	$12,959.10	$12,393.13	$565.97	4.57%
							$133,668.45	$124,931.22	$8,737.23	6.99%

We finally invested our money in August 2017 so in order to get the full year picture we need to wait until August 2018 to get the accurate annual return, but as far as it goes it's great.

There are two significant lessons to learn here:

1) Even if the annual return stays exactly as it is today – that's still great. Bank deposit rates are in the range of 1%-2% so the investments have already outperformed anything there. And also this has been completely passive for us, and that's invaluable when we both have other things to do with our time.

And, the most significant learning is:

2) This Tier Two portfolio really, really is a long term overall strategy, and you have to have the control to leave it alone and not get overexcited or panic.

If we look at each portfolio we can see some shares that are massively down by 40% or so and then to offset that some shares that are 40% up. But overall the portfolio is up and that's what this strategy does: it takes an overall, look at a small selection of shares which, over time, produce 10% or more per year, but there are times where you just have to hold your nerve with it.

There is no point selling the high performer or the low performer at any time between the annual review dates because in order to do the strategy properly and get the returns that the strategy creates you have to follow it like a slave. You can change the rules of the strategy if you want to (and say, sell when a share increases or decreases by a certain amount) but that would then be a different – and untested – strategy.

The lesson then is to stick with the strategy: it's tried and tested – leave it alone!

And then timing.

There have been times in the year when this portfolio has been down and there have been times in the year (see the portfolios below) when they have been well above where they are now, and that's OK.

The portfolios printed below (nearing the end of 2017) show the UK portion up by nearly 12% and the US portion up by just under 9% – so at some stage in our year we did get the 10% – and more.

Edit columns   Refresh Prices   Print 🖨 Export 📤   🔍 Search

Symbol	Links		Qty	Description	▲ Price	Price Change £	Price Change %	Market Value	Book Cost	Gain / Loss £	Gain / Loss %
AZN	Buy Sell	⚙ 🔗 ⓘ	221	ASTRAZENECA ORD USD0.25	5,485.00p	22.50p	0.41%	£12,121.85	£10,132.34	£1,989.51	19.64%
BP.	Buy Sell	⚙ 🔗 ⓘ	2318	BP ORD USD0.25	567.90p	0.40p	0.07%	£13,163.92	£10,333.29	£2,830.63	27.39%
BT.A	Buy Sell	⚙ 🔗 ⓘ	3374	BT GROUP ORD GBP0.05	295.90p	-2.45p	-0.82%	£9,983.67	£10,340.19	£-356.52	-3.45%
GSK	Buy Sell	⚙ 🔗 ⓘ	672	GLAXOSMITHKLINE ORD GBP0.25	1,463.40p	5.40p	0.37%	£9,834.05	£10,236.37	£-402.32	-3.93%
HSBA	Buy Sell	⚙ 🔗 ⓘ	1360	HSBC HOLDINGS PLC ORD USD0.50	844.70p	-4.70p	-0.55%	£11,487.92	£10,188.83	£1,299.09	12.75%
IMB	Buy Sell	⚙ 🔗 ⓘ	297	IMPERIAL BRANDS PLC ORD GBP0.10	3,289.50p	-55.00p	-1.64%	£9,769.82	£10,188.04	£-418.22	-4.11%
NG.	Buy Sell	⚙ 🔗 ⓘ	1080	NATIONAL GRID ORD GBP0.12431289	894.10p	-12.76p	-1.41%	£9,656.28	£10,159.10	£-502.82	-4.95%
RDSA	Buy Sell	⚙ 🔗 ⓘ	471	ROYAL DUTCH SHELL 'A'SHS EUR0.07(GBP)	2,710.00p	-3.60p	-0.11%	£12,764.10	£9,980.75	£2,783.35	27.89%
RDSB	Buy Sell	⚙ 🔗 ⓘ	481	ROYAL DUTCH SHELL 'B'ORD EUR0.07	2,825.00p	1.00p	0.04%	£13,588.25	£10,292.21	£3,296.04	32.02%
VOD	Buy Sell	⚙ 🔗 ⓘ	4522	VODAFONE GROUP ORD USD0.2095238	250.40p	2.05p	0.81%	£11,323.09	£9,998.43	£1,324.66	13.25%
								£113,692.95	£101,849.55	£11,843.40	11.63%

UK Markets prices delayed by 15 min or more

Edit columns   Refresh Prices

Print 🖶 Export 📄 🔍 Search

Symbol	Links	Qty	Description	Price	Price Change £	%	Market Value	Book Cost	Gain / Loss £	%
AZN	Buy Sell £ ✗ i	227	ASTRAZENECA ORD USD0.25	5,127.00p	44.00p	0.87%	£11,638.29	£10,425.46	£1,212.83	11.63%
BP.	Buy Sell £ ✗ i	2351	BP ORD USD0.25	532.00p	-5.40p	-1.00%	£12,507.32	£10,499.15	£2,008.17	19.13%
BT.A	Buy Sell £ ✗ i	3442	BT GROUP ORD GBP0.05	251.60p	3.62p	1.46%	£8,660.07	£10,502.16	-£1,842.09	-17.54%
GSK	Buy Sell £ ✗ i	682	GLAXOSMITHKLINE ORD GBP0.25	1,472.20p	7.14p	0.49%	£10,040.40	£10,379.30	-£338.90	-3.27%
HSBA	Buy Sell £ ✗ i	1389	HSBC HOLDINGS PLC ORD USD0.50	729.70p	10.20p	1.42%	£10,135.53	£10,386.43	-£250.90	-2.42%
IMB	Buy Sell £ ✗ i	303	IMPERIAL BRANDS PLC GBP0.10	2,628.00p	14.00p	0.54%	£7,962.84	£10,341.38	-£2,378.54	-23.00%
NG.	Buy Sell £ ✗ i	1080	NATIONAL GRID ORD GBP0.12431289	849.70p	8.04p	0.96%	£9,176.76	£10,159.10	-£982.34	-9.67%
RDSA	Buy Sell £ ✗ i	471	ROYAL DUTCH SHELL 'A' SHS EUR0.07(GBP)	2,520.00p	-11.50p	-0.45%	£11,869.20	£9,980.75	£1,888.45	18.92%
RDSB	Buy Sell £ ✗ i	488	ROYAL DUTCH SHELL 'B' ORD EUR0.07	2,586.00p	-9.90p	-0.38%	£12,619.68	£10,451.80	£2,167.88	20.74%
VOD	Buy Sell £ ✗ i	4615	VODAFONE GROUP ORD USD0.2095238	213.50p	3.00p	1.43%	£9,853.03	£10,189.61	-£336.58	-3.30%
							£104,463.12	£103,315.14	£1,147.98	1.11%

303

Timing

If we consider the extremes of portfolio value so far then it appears that the issue of timing IS important, and I never thought it was. However the timing issue is this:

It doesn't matter when you get in and invest because that's your starting date – but it DOES matter when you sell and get out.

The final lesson for us then is invest as soon as you can but don't get desperate or fixated about when you're going to sell, because that day *may* matter – but in all honesty it probably won't because the longer this portfolio is left to do its thing (with its annual review of course), then any dips and wobbles will be less significant.

Leave this for the medium to long term and if your plan is to sell then just watch the values more carefully for a month or two before you sell up.

Conclusion

And that's all folks!

Michael and I started this experiment in May 2017 and had a plan to learn how to invest – and trade – to generate a 10% return on or money and by doing so, secure our long term financial future.

We've now achieved that and have set up funds for our future pensions. And interestingly, we've done that just on the share investing part of the portfolio.

We now know that we can make that return a lot higher if we **trade** with some of the money as well. But we don't need to do that if we don't want to. Therefore, the investments we've made can be easily done by every man, woman and child anywhere in the world with very small amounts of starting capital.

And what's more important is that these simple investing strategies from Tiers One and Two of our Pyramid are ENOUGH to generate that 10% return and are ENOUGH to provide long term security and wealth for all – that's one hell of a statement.

We now know that we could solve the UK (and other countries) pensions crisis if only we could convince the government to follow these simple steps for every child being born, but sadly, that could never happen – but what CAN happen is that each parent can take responsibility and do it for their own child – and themselves, of course. Let's all do that!

Daily Diary

Gill: On the one hand, I'm relieved that this one year experiment is over but on the other hand, I'm delighted with the results and what we've achieved and I know we won't stop now. I genuinely believe that we have something here (and we also now have the evidence) that could be a game changer in the way that people look at their bigger long term financial picture. This one simple set of strategies could generate financial security for all for all their lives – what an extraordinary achievement that would be.

And thanks, Mike!

Michael: Now that this is over (or not) I'm sort of annoyed that I didn't start earlier. It's been an absolute no-brainer, because of how easy it's been for such a passive reward that future financial security provides.

Thanks for reading and hopefully you can now start investing yourself.

Postscript: 8th August 2018

Although we started this learning and investing project on the 1st May 2017, it did take us a couple of months to get to grips with enough of the basics to feel knowledgeable enough to start to invest, and that learning has been reported elsewhere.

As a consequence I didn't actually transfer my investment money of £197,825 into a broker account until the 29th of June 2017.

The initial cash investment

Settlement Date	Date	Description	Credit	Running Balance
29/06/2017	29/06/2017	Funds Received 28.06.17	£197,825.00	£197,825.00

And then it took another couple of weeks to get the stocks selected and the money invested, and the UK portion of the funds was invested on the 1st August:

Settlement Date	Date	Symbol	Sedol	Description	Reference	Debit	Cre
02/08/2017	31/07/2017	AZN	0989529	218 ASTRAZENE Del 45.54 S Date 02/08/17	KFSGQ2	£9,983.68	
01/08/2017	28/07/2017	BP.	0798059	2251 BP Del 4.41 S Date 01/08/17	KFRXWJ	£9,998.35	
01/08/2017	28/07/2017	NG.	BDR05C0	1061 NATL GRID Del 9.37 S Date 01/08/17	KFRXVX	£9,997.25	
01/08/2017	28/07/2017	GSK	0925288	655 GLAXOSMIT Del 15.16 S Date 01/08/17	KFRWZM	£9,990.40	
01/08/2017	28/07/2017	HSBA	0540528	1334 HSBC HLDG Del 7.45 S Date 01/08/17	KFRWVK	£9,995.96	
01/08/2017	28/07/2017	BT.A	3091357	3256 BT GROU Del 3.05 S Date 01/08/17	KFRWSC	£9,999.17	
01/08/2017	28/07/2017	VOD	BH4HKS3	4522 VODE GROU Del 2.19 S Date 01/08/17	KFRWQ2	£9,998.43	
01/08/2017	28/07/2017	IMB	0454492	290 IMPL BRAN Del 34.19 S Date 01/08/17	KFRW6F	£9,972.11	
01/08/2017	28/07/2017	RDSB	B03MM40	468 ROYAL DUT'B' Del 21.21 S Date 01/08/17	KFRW5G	£9,984.26	
01/08/2017	28/07/2017	RDSA	B03MLX2	471 ROYAL DUTCH'A' Del 21.07 S Date 01/08/17	KFRW4F	£9,980.75	

Then I converted funds into dollars for the US purchases on the 23rd August.

23/08/2017   21/08/2017   97924 POUNDS STERLING NoTf 1.27 S   KF6MVR   £97,924.64
                            Date 23/08/17

And so here we are broadly one year later on the 8th August 2018, being a suitable date in between the UK and US investment days in 2017.

IF this learning and planning has worked my fund needs to be worth:

£197,825 + 10% ie £217,607.50p

But, as you can see from the download below, my fund is actually worth **£218,757.12!**

| | Total Value £218,757.12 | | Total Cash £3,990.24 | | Total Investments £214,766.88 |

I've inserted below the front sheet of my fund portfolio account showing the full amount and the date – 8th August 2018 – in the bottom corner of the screen.

www.financialinvestingandtrading.com

US Markets Closing Prices

Edit columns   Refresh Prices

Print 🖶   Export 📄   🔍 Search

Symbol	Links	Qty	Description	Price $	Price Change $	Price Change %	Market Value	Book Cost	Gain / Loss $	Gain / Loss %	Corp Action
CVX	Buy Sell 📊 ↗ ℹ	115	CHEVRON CORPORATION COM USD0.75	$125.18	$0.00	0.00%	$14,395.70	$12,514.03	$1,881.67	15.04%	
CSCO	Buy Sell 📊 ↗ ℹ	390	CISCO SYSTEMS INC COM USD0.001	$43.58	n/a	n/a	$16,996.20	$12,468.28	$4,527.92	36.32%	
KO	Buy Sell 📊 ↗ ℹ	265	COCA-COLA CO COM USD0.25	$46.50	$0.00	0.00%	$12,322.50	$12,144.50	$178.00	1.47%	
XOM	Buy Sell 📊 ↗ ℹ	160	EXXON MOBIL CORPORATION COM NPV	$81.27	$0.00	0.00%	$13,003.20	$12,498.98	$504.22	4.03%	
GE	Buy Sell 📊 ↗ ℹ	495	GENERAL ELECTRIC CO COM USD0.06	$13.16	$0.00	0.00%	$6,514.20	$12,491.68	-$5,977.48	-47.85%	
INTC	Buy Sell 📊 ↗ ℹ	345	INTEL CORP COM USD0.001	$49.70	$0.00	0.00%	$17,146.50	$12,531.28	$4,615.22	36.83%	
IBM	Buy Sell 📊 ↗ ℹ	90	INTERNATIONAL BUS MACH CORP COM USD0.20	$147.01	$0.00	0.00%	$13,230.90	$12,837.28	$393.62	3.07%	
MRK	Buy Sell 📊 ↗ ℹ	200	MERCK & CO INC COM USD0.50	$66.58	$0.00	0.00%	$13,316.00	$12,541.78	$774.22	6.17%	
PFE	Buy Sell 📊 ↗ ℹ	375	PFIZER INC COM USD0.05	$40.84	$0.00	0.00%	$15,315.00	$12,510.28	$2,804.72	22.42%	
VZ	Buy Sell 📊 ↗ ℹ	255	VERIZON COMMUNICATIONS COM USD0.10	$52.46	$0.00	0.00%	$13,377.30	$12,393.13	$984.17	7.94%	
							$135,617.50	$124,931.22	$10,686.28	8.55%	

Show 20 ▼ entries   First Previous 1 Next Last

Conclusion

Therefore I can, without any doubt whatsoever, conclude that this normal mum and son have successfully learnt in one year, the skills required to generate at least 10% over a year on investments that can be selected in less than an hour.

In fact we generated:

£218,757 - £197,825 = £20,932 ie **10.58%.**

And as long as we keep doing that year in and year out – our orginal plan of financial freedom and a pension for each of us is a certainty!